A Punishment for Peace

By the same author: NO MORE STRANGERS

A Punishment
for Peace

Philip Berrigan, S.S.J.

THE MACMILLAN COMPANY

COLLIER-MACMILLAN LTD., LONDON

The author wishes to acknowledge the following for permission to reproduce copyrighted material: Marion Morehouse Cummings, Harcourt, Brace & World, Inc., and MacGibbon and Kee Ltd., for *no thanks*, #54, by E. E. Cummings, copyright © 1935 by E. E. Cummings, renewed 1963 by Marion Morehouse Cummings, reprinted from *Poems 1923-1954* by E. E. Cummings; John Beecher for an extract from *To Live and Die in Dixie* by John Beecher, published by Red Mountain Editions, 1966; Grove Press, Inc., for extracts from *The Wretched of the Earth* by Frantz Fanon, translated from the French by Constance Farrington, copyright © 1963 by Presence Africaine; Clarence Major, for "Vietnam #4" by Clarence Major, published in *Where Is Vietnam?: American Poets Respond* (Doubleday & Company, Inc.), edited by Walter Lowenfels, copyright © 1967 by Walter Lowenfels; Richmond Lattimore and *The New Republic*, for "Report from a Planet" by Richmond Lattimore, copyright © 1967 by Harrison-Blaine of New Jersey, Inc.

Copyright © 1969 by Philip Berrigan, S.S.J.

Library of Congress Catalog Card Number: 78-77969

FIRST PRINTING

The Macmillan Company
Collier-Macmillan Canada Ltd., Toronto, Ontario

Printed in the United States of America

1486315

To my mother and father, who in giving me life
never asked a refund for themselves,

<mark>AND</mark>

to my partners in "crime" at Catonsville, Maryland,
on May 17, 1968. I have met no better Christians:
Father Daniel Berrigan, Brother David Darst,
John Hogan, Thomas Lewis, Marjorie Bradford Melville,
Thomas Melville, George Mische, and Mary Moylan.

CONTENTS

I.   CONSENSUS SOCIETY! CONSENSUS CHURCH?   1

II.   THE COLOR OF POVERTY   27

III.   THE FIRE THIS TIME?   57

IV.   IMPERIALISM, THE GOLDEN RULE OF PEACE   83

V.   COLD-WAR ASPIRATIONS AND SECRETS   112

VI.   REFLECTIONS ON CHURCH-STATE COVENANTS   145

      EPILOGUE   171

      NOTES   175

ACKNOWLEDGMENTS

My gratitude to Dan—for example, love, editing, all without limit. To Marilyn and Bill O'Connor for friendship, hospitality, editing, for anything required.

To Lillian Moulden for putting up with mistakes and endless typing. To Herbert Marcuse for *One-Dimensional Man*. To Carl Oglesby for his essays in *Containment and Change*. To William A. Williams for his *Tragedy of American Diplomacy*.

To my friends and enemies for supplying their minds, their time, their honesty. All of which helped me to reality.

"On him lies a punishment that brings us peace, and through his wounds we are healed."

—I<small>SAIAS</small> 53:5

"There will be no peace without justice, no justice without love, no love without Christ. The punishment for peace accepted by Him must now become our own."

—A<small>NONYMOUS</small>

I

Consensus Society! Consensus Church?

Jehovah buried, Satan dead,
do fearers worship Much and Quick;
badness not being felt as bad,
itself thinks goodness what is meek;
obey says toc, submit says tic,
Eternity's a Five Year Plan:
if Joy with Pain shall hang in hock
who dares to call himself a man?

go dreamless knaves on Shadows fed,
your Harry's Tom, your Tom is Dick;
while Gadgets murder squawk and add,
the cult of Same is all the chic;
by instruments, both span and spic,
are justly measured Spic and Span:
to kiss the mike if Jew turn kike
who dares to call himself a man?

loudly for Truth have liars pled,
their heels for Freedom slaves will click;
where Boobs are holy, poets mad,
illustrious punks of Progress shriek;

when Souls are outlawed, Hearts are sick,
Hearts being sick, Minds nothing can:
if Hate's a game and Love's a φυκ
who dares to call himself a man

Why? Because, this world is all abeak;
and lifepreservers there are none:
and waves which only He may walk
Who dares to call Himself a man.
                    —E. E. CUMMINGS, *no thanks,* #54

"WHO DARES TO CALL HIMSELF A MAN?"—A GOOD
question, full of possibilities for all, full of fascination, indictment,
terror, liberation. A question asked equally in stock exchange and
hovel, rectory and bistro, asked in so many ways as to sometimes
obscure or lose itself. No "lifepreservers," only "waves," and the
example of Him who walked them, "Who dares to call Himself a
Man."

All of which may chart the direction of belief while helping
little with its content. One must accept the "waves." For at the
point of walking, society now supplies what nature used to terrify
Peter: enticement, confusion, deception, threat, and finally a drawing into itself, assimilation. And what one may look to as the
strong arm of Christ, the Church, is so often like the waves and
like the sea. No help from that quarter. In fact, the Church sometimes makes climbing from the trough more difficult.

With that, perhaps the analogy may be laid to rest. Western
society, under the guise of evolving and ennobling benefactor,
stands today as the enemy of man. It has effectively suspended
freedom, making man both victim and operating cog. Objects of
belief (God and man) have undergone a substitution; man believes in the technological apparatus that so titillates, insensitizes,
and rewards him. Western society has become both idol and dic-
tator, hope and inflexible director of life.

Within this context religion, more often than not, is servant of
the engulfing whole, the technological society itself. Marx's view

of religion as the opium of the people is now loaded with a meaning tremendously more dangerous than his intent: Religion secures people to the system and does it in the name of God. It has become, all too willingly, a kind of ethical adhesive which combines with profit, law and order, consumer rewards, and national pride to keep the machinery from breaking down or running low. Religion, indeed, offers two valuable ingredients for the efficient operation of a technocracy: moral incentive and moral sanction.

Roughly, such is the believer's position in the new totalitarianism of the West, particularly of America. *Freedom* has become a bankrupt word, devoid of most of its meaning, part of a general rhetoric of despair—and in comparison with Christian freedom, very nearly an obscenity. In any valid sense, freedom is not allowed. It is not suppressed (such would be a crude attack upon the assumption of its presence); it is rather finessed, bought off, ridiculed, and finally absorbed. One who questions, dissents, or stands for qualitative alternatives is shown quickly and forcibly that his time and effort are the epitome of witlessness—that he is quite simply a fool whose irresponsibility is jeopardizing the "common" good. Believers (as well as all others) are therefore forced to submit to peace through nuclear stalemate, an illogic justified by the logic of a consumer society; forced to conclude that "freedom's" price tag is self-determination's guarantee in South Vietnam (or in Guatemala, Colombia, Ecuador, and Peru); forced to agree that consumer "health" receives its richest vitamins from defense and war, which make it capable of satisfying both the war machine with guns and the rich with butter, though the bread for the poor might be scarce; forced to suspect that when religion blesses war or remains silent before its atrocities or speaks but does not act, religion is being given a new gospel by the rationality of the system, new wineskins being used to replace old.

It is not accident, therefore, that alternate modes and institutions of life more conducive to human integrity are scarcely imagined in a technological society like our own, let alone implemented. The national "establishment," with all its satraps—economic, political, and religious institutions is almost inherently

resistant to change in its value system, rationale, and operation.
As cause, the value system is consumer mystique; as effect, it is
way of life. Both are reciprocal, self-reinforcing, self-perpetuating.
Both are secure, sensual, undemanding, they promise more, and
promise it more quickly

If change is tolerated at all, it is welcomed in virtue of the
status quo, through improved scientific research and technique,
for example, which stimulate productive efficiency, improve "defense," and heighten standards of living, thereby making the *status
quo* more and better. Humanistic change, on the contrary—even of
such obvious need and promise as human rights, antipoverty, and
peace—is found at variance with establishment suppositions and
as such is given lip service (antipoverty), co-option (human
rights), or opposition (peace).

One ventures such criticism with trepidation; the sheer complexity of American life very nearly defies analysis. More importantly, such criticism is made in light of the enormous
accomplishments of our society, which has in times past harbored
the desperate and poor, and in times present opened awesome
and marvelous vistas of freedom from want and drudgery through
the laboratory and machine.

Similar thoughts strike one in assessing current liabilities and
assets in the Church, which is, with all the seriousness and sincerity it can muster, trying to come to terms with both the Gospel
and the world—and doing this (as a further claim upon sympathy) as it moves into the first stages of theological upheaval,
depleted membership and personnel, slackening revenues, and
abandoned institutions. For both society and Church, life's dilemmas today are bewildering and torturous, and in face of them,
does one construct or destroy, serve or weaken, by laying bare
the sores, by building a backlog of questions that are sometimes
premature, abrupt, or presently unanswerable?

The only retort that can be offered, I suppose, is a view of man.
One hopes for man because Christ became man, and because one
has seen man live in the community of friends and in the heroism
of poor and colored people. Because, too, one has caught the
breath of the great men of our age: John XXIII, Teilhard de

Chardin, the Kennedy brothers, Buber, Schweitzer, Hammarskjöld, even Russell, U Thant, and De Gaulle. Man can be man in the spirit of these men; he need not be a fratricide or a parasite or a universal Nazi—one who cedes mind and heart to architects of terror and debasement, only to plead obedience later at an accounting. Man, after all, needs very little to be man: He needs necessities for sustenance, community for friendship, room for contribution, hope of acceptance on both sides of the grave.

Such a view clashes harshly with the reality of an America whose incomparable power is greater than that of all humanity combined and compared. In fact, the clash of possibility and fact leaves one sodden with misery, searching desperately for human and divine excuses to explain such rape of potential, such monumental waste, such unhappiness and barbarity in the midst of plenty. For America's power can neither accept its blacks, nor succor its poor, nor assure its peace, nor answer the starvation of millions abroad. America's power is tragically isolated from wisdom, sickly moralized, and immorally moral; it is a power so immense and arrogant that it dictates its end to those who wield it, making them men of power who are mere means to its ends. America's power is, finally, a threat that keeps the world unnerved and aghast, that has in large measure defined the course of the cold war and nuclear brinksmanship, and that may in all probability bring mankind to the final idiocy of World War III.

At the minimum, such power must be scrutinized, tested, even withstood. To a sobering extent, it is incapable of evaluating itself in this way; the men who serve it are caught within its toils and, in fact, have become its creatures. (The credibility gap from Washington or protests of "patriotism" from the Dow Chemical Company are proof enough of this.) Moreover, such power is even now perfecting its own dynamics and increasing its own momentum, for it must vindicate itself in the face of growing appetites at home and proliferating enemies abroad.

Most importantly, any critical theory of American and/or Western society cannot exclude the Church from notice. For the Christian, it is infinitely more important that the Church be faithful than his country be just. If one believes, therefore, that

the Church is the instrument of Christ's redemption, the community of God's Spirit, the protector of the poor, the critic of
injustice, and the advocate of mercy, it cannot well be overlooked. Here again the gap between conception and fact impels
one to notice, and to ask intensely, What is so wrong with the
Church that it could permit a professedly Christian country to
so decline into sophisticated barbarism? This much is becoming
clear: If America continues to tear itself to pieces at home while
continuing to export its violence abroad, such will have been
possible because the Church had gone into a prosperous somnolence at the expense of the Gospel and the Cross.

Any critique of American society must proceed directly from
the question, What is wrong? As we shall see, part of the difficulty in coming to agreement as to "what is wrong" is that
Americans largely reject the question in favor of its converse,
What is right? or What is better? What is right is a spiraling
gross national product, middle- and upper-class unanimity of aim,
nearly worldwide economic presence, superpower status un-
matched in world history, domestic proliferation of goods and
services, more jobs, schools, libraries, TV's, and airconditioners,
more food, alcohol, and tobacco. What is wrong is the price paid
for what is considered right: a swollen defense economy, world
police action, peace through overkill capacity, a nearly autonomous military establishment, a gratuitous and stupid foreign war,
persistent unemployment, black turbulence, white-black poverty,
rotting cities, poisoned air and water. When Americans are con-
fronted with "what is wrong," there is not so much the tendency
to ignore evidence or to discount wholly its importance as there
is the unbalanced tendency to consider the liabilities of the American Way of Life as a small evil in a package of great good. And
the rejoinder invariably finds expression in personal-national
terms: "So what? Nothing's perfect! We never had it so good!"
   In addition, any critique of society must go deeper to pose the
"why" of "what is wrong?" It is the "why" that obscures the na-

tional judgment, discourages nonconformity, and prevents people from dissent, protest, and *integrity*.

When material needs are primary, men become tied, by and large, to the process of satisfying them. More than that, they invariably become part of that process and a ready defender of it. The higher one's satisfaction or scale of possession, the greater the allegiance expected by the process. Self-interest has been appealed to; self-interest demands a response. One has stepped into the circle, and if the circle is not vicious, it is indeed sad.

If, therefore, the technology that now controls society causes growing prosperity year by year, and if prosperity is reflected in enhanced income and status, one's problematic situation deepens and one stills proportionately the voice of doubt. If, furthermore, material, cultural, and social needs are constantly redefined and reemphasized by the communications media (salesmen as they are for the consumer economy), one's dilemma grows. In a word, the apparent rationality of all the addenda feeding the "sweet life" contains, muffles, and even silences the irrational human cost paid for them. Such irreconcilables meet in persons who are notable successes in the system but utter failures as human beings.

Such irreconcilables meet in the nation also: growing productivity tied to growing destructive capacity; brinksmanship as a policy for peace; an Asian war that no one can convincingly defend morally, legally, or politically; calculated misery in the face of staggering wealth; and the surrender of responsibility, judgment, and decision to elite centers of power. Caesar's bread and circuses are now offered in only slightly different form—as the bourgeois trappings of modern life, which in digestion provoke more greed than fulfillment.

The first heady promise of scientism and technology was the control of nature and its reduction to human service. But who was to control technology but technocrats (people)? Somewhere along the line the leash slipped—technology ravaged nature to stuff people with nature's goods. Scientific control has ended in the scientific control of man.

One could justifiably call this a form of totalitarianism, a

fascism springing not from a political system but from technological rationality. Social control is achieved not by repressing
fundamental rights but by first creating appetites, then manip-
ulating them, then producing to satisfy the needs so assiduously
cultivated. As long as products can meet promises so long will
consumers be satisfied, and controlled. Government itself is not
exempt from power domination by productive enterprise, which
is relentlessly forcing the political order to front for its interests.
In other words, commonweal as a political concept is increasingly
indistinguishable from a glutted consumer market kept tractable
and passive through the satiation of (largely) false needs. In
this sense, political power cannot be isolated from the economic
power that sponsors it, since the machine (now the computer?)
is the standard power behind political parties and all politicians.
And no party can remain viable on the American scene without
being emphatically in favor of driving industrial capacity to its
limits. Logically and progressively, a welfare state of the magnitude of our own becomes a warfare state as well.

This subtle and creeping totalitarianism can be regarded
through another lens. By any sort of absolute right, a man's needs
cease beyond what is required to make life livable: food, shelter,
clothing (in a wealthy economy like our own, adequate education, decent income [guaranteed, if necessary], security in sickness and in old age). Ideally, society owes its members a reasonable share of what it can produce for their human enhancement
as free, responsible citizens. They in turn have the obligation to
see that their society remains responsible and free.

"Free" becomes, in such a discussion, a critical concept and
a practicality. In American society freedom is somehow separated
from humanism. Freedom is somehow separated from an education calculated to prepare one to serve life rather than to serve a
system. Freedom is somehow separated from a view of people
as people rather than as stereotypes of class or race. Freedom is
somehow separated from the mysterious chemistry that makes a
man—truth, justice, compassion, integrity.

Quality and universality are dangerously reprobate as human
attributes, since one has to be lonely and exposed to cultivate

them. Though one can follow an individual and largely solitary course to cut through the turgid conformism of establishment habits, the social cost is enormous.

"Freedom," under analysis, rather means the pressures exerted from childhood toward the creation of a passive and somewhat stupefied agent of a mechanically dominated society. "Freedom" means victimization by a value system projected from every conceivable institution and experience: family, school, church, government, profession or job, recreation, press and television. "Freedom" means the repetitious and lifelong acceptance of determining and dominating forces that tend of necessity to suffocate or eliminate qualitative choice and movement.

If one is free to choose at all, it is within areas defined by a consumer-war economy: schools more or less inferior; draft, reserve, or education until overage; one occupation or another whose benefit is more operational than human; suburban boxes and squares of lawn or apartment ghettos in the central city; this or that vacation, depending on one's status; cars obsolescent before they are driven; and on and on. Freedom is reductively the suck and shove to become the tiny edition of larger society, to be mediocre or to excel in pragmatism, power sensitivity, neuroses, prejudices, moral confusion, and unconscious hypocrisy.

The value attached by Americans to such "freedoms" can be judged both by the near obsessiveness with which they are discussed and by the quality of discussion. On the human level "freedoms" are preponderantly dealt with in terms of threats to them, such as poor and black people, Communist belligerence, De Gaulle's ingratitude, unrest over delayed victory in Vietnam, black anarchy in the Congo. On the material level "freedoms" center on the relative merits of split-level or ranch house, country club or public course, or a choice of deodorant, bourbon, and laundry soap. The real world suffers constantly a torturous molding into the world of affluence; it is accepted if it enhances affluence, rejected if it does not. Yet convictions persist that this is freedom, this is life, and these "things" are the stuff of life.

Consequently, domination is not applied by conventional means of state control, not by inhibiting speech, censoring the press, restricting association and religious practice. Repressions of social creativity and true individuality are far more scientific, and effective. Government controls (conventional totalitarianism), technolog ional controls, are covert and imperceptible. Marketing techniques aim to articulate superfluous needs as real needs, false needs as necessities. Marketing appeal is aimed at illusions of health, appearance, acceptability, status, and solidarity, reinforced by a value network that makes the appeal reasonable, persuasive, and credible. If the result is a kind of pandering, this is justified through references to the good of the whole, with its impressive achievements of prosperity and power, its ability to compete with other societies, and so forth.

The marketing message deals blatantly with human needs as though they had no limit, as though, indeed, needs should be expanded as far as advertising genius can take them, as far as claims for them can be made credible. The object of sales is clearly to save people from thinking and, moreover, to have them feel dissatisfaction with present ownership, or absence of ownership. The pitch is then made in such a way that, implicitly, a better version of life arrives with possession of the product.

In terms of control or attempts to control, the technological process (research, production, and sales) is obviously not involved in a conspiracy to rob people of their humanity. Scientists, production-line chiefs, and Madison Avenue executives hardly consider the good or ill impact of their product upon the consumer. The net effect, however, is control of the public, since profit motivation verges on obsession, and obsession shows itself in the disavowal of moral responsibility beyond the product itself.

The regulation of people is, consequently, implicit in the need capitalism has to disgorge its overproductivity upon an already overfed, overclothed, overapplianced, and overstimulated market. To keep people buying, extremes of absurdity and bad taste become commonplace—in fact, the whole intellectual and moral desert of television is intended to condition buying. Profits are America's golden calf, and nothing short of an earthquake or God's judgment must interfere with them.

This is not to suggest that irresponsibility in this matter is a one-way street, and that the consumer is a passive, guiltless victim. On the contrary, Americans are enthusiastic buyers; the marketing world is precisely designed to exploit their joyful and virtuous delight in goods. They are also tireless, if unconscious, salesmen; no little portion of their waking hours is spent defending or selling their possessions to their friends. What women wear, what men drive, what unusual sense experience has been recently undergone, all are subjects of interminable and exhaustive conversations. "Things," it is generally assumed, have much to do with making a person, a society, a nation—America is great precisely because it has used its wealth ("things") generously and boldly.

Consumer buying or salesmanship, however, causes more than profit for the wider society. It promotes an identification with both product and producer—in fact, with both the rationale and the machinery of the industrial society. Social psychologists would call this phenomenon mimesis, or a feeling of oneness with mass production, mass distribution, and mass consumption. A claim has been put upon the entire person, even upon those mysterious inner spaces that a man usually reserves for himself and for God. These have been invaded and reduced, so that identification is made not with oneself but with society as a whole, with the technological monolith. One does not become a spectator to its complexity or an awestruck and horrified judge; one becomes instead a microcosm of it—a servant-promoter, if you will.

Such intense and undiscerning involvement militates against the development of critical reason and keeps it immobile at infantile levels. Reason, judgment, volition, and emotional life are kept at a plateau of bondage to establishment values and mores, and appeals neither to reason nor morality are likely to disturb their fixations. It is utterly consistent, therefore, that the public accepts packaging as more important than content in food, rust on a year-old car as reason to get a new one, or an influx of Negroes as an automatic threat to property rights.

Essentially, the problem becomes one of violence, a systematic offense against truth and justice. Violence bombards individuals from most quarters of society and during most of one's waking

hours. It is received, assimilated, and returned again to its source.
Yet it leaves its mark, and its damage can take the form of in-
difference, boredom, sporadic use of time and effort, uncertainty,
inability to foster an enduring friendship, periodic or habitual
misuse of others. Social patterns have become personal patterns,
leaving society further entrapped and leaving persons further
baffled, ineffective, and despairing.

The human product is, to use Herbert Marcuse's apt description, one-dimensional man, who expresses himself in one-dimensional thought and behavior. Vertical relationships to God and
self have all been subsumed by a horizontal relationship to in-
dustrialized society which controls one as cog and patron. Within
such limits, if concepts are not pragmatic and operational, if they
do not serve established systems, they tend to face rejection, on
one extreme as subversive or "communistic" and on the other, as
simply useless.

Two examples of the tyrannical control of system over thought
come to mind. The first involves a suggestion by me to a Congressman friend that testimony by economists be given before
the Senate Foreign Relations Committee regarding: (1) the real
extent of American economic presence abroad; (2) the proportion of the gross national product dependent upon such investments; (3) alleged collusion between investments and American
militarism in these areas.

Such a request seemed both logical and necessary, since mili-
tary-industrial alliances consume about seven-tenths of tax dollars, and since it is predictable that a wedding so mutually
satisfactory in America be energetically consummated abroad as
well. In a word, if America must have markets for its surpluses
and must have foreign resources and labor to feed a mounting
desire for profit and prosperity, it must have a political policy to
favor such interests, and arms to defend them.

The Congressman answered in typically sympathetic and
forthright fashion. He agreed with the necessity for such investigation, and to substantiate his own awareness, recalled a visit he
made to Peru, where some four hundred American corporations
had holdings. Yet he reluctantly refused to be involved in over-

tures to the chairman of the committee, Senator J. William Fulbright. There were the Congressman's own preoccupations, to be sure, but he thought the enterprise too "explosive" and felt that it would hardly be regarded as otherwise by Fulbright.

Another example was a recent "think tank" sponsored by the American Friends Service Committee in Philadelphia. A good representative spectrum of liberal Democrats was there: a governor (other politicians invited declined the risk of appearance), two former ambassadors (one American and one foreign), several important editors and commentators, a former head of a major civil-rights organization, a priest, a minister, and a rabbi. In a word, progressive elements of the establishment were in attendance, and all were involved in opposition to the Vietnam war.

It soon became apparent that little agreement reigned as to the significance of this war to Vietnam, to America, and to the world. In characteristically human fashion, the tragedy of Vietnam was laid on the table not in its own terms or in terms of the broader danger to mankind, but according to personal experience and position within the power structure. Few comprehended, apparently, the human factors of the war: What were Vietnamese rights? Why did America need this war? What moral and legal obligations bound this country in light of possible wider war, and World War III? Because no priority was given moral and human concerns, there could be no talk of unilateral withdrawal, of civil disobedience, or of revolution. In the end two measures were adopted, both of them framework policies. The first was to attempt to establish a news agency intended to supply communications media with a truer version of Vietnam realities than that supplied by the Government. The second aimed through political organization to preserve the Democratic Party in power and to produce a peace candidate, ending the war that way.

Not so strangely, the only people present who questioned such provisions on the ground that they did not meet issues were those who had served the black and the poor in radical movements, who knew something of human rights and what an adequate response to those rights should be, who had felt the black (now the Vietnamese) plight under American castes of privilege. True,

a day-long conference was too short a time to plunge into complicated and elusive issues. Yet I am fairly convinced that time
was not the problem; attitudes were. Most men there had an unconscious yet complete commitment to functional codes, and it
made hardly any difference that their interpretation of such
codes tended to be liberal.

There are many reasons why men mobilize, many causes around
which they can be mobilized. Hate, love, fear, greed—any combination of these or a combination of all—inspire causes that testify
to life or bring it to ruin. It is really quite simple: Give men a
cause, prod their noble or base emotions, and one has a movement, or a war. Technological society, however, mobilizes through
plenty and the defense of plenty, becoming in the process not
only the welfare, but the warfare, state as well. Patterns of mobilization follow these rough lines: Produce consumer products
as extravagantly as possible in order to sell them extravagantly
(free enterprise); match overproduction with overadvertising to
cause overconsumption; hunt markets overseas to unload surpluses; exploit foreign labor and resources to feed the native
industrial maw; meanwhile, articulate a threat to both foreign
aggrandizement and home prosperity (Communism), and build
a military machine to meet it.

Loyalty, fear, and greed are alternately stimulated by en-
comiums to national prestige, by revelations of enemy efforts to
outstrip us, by promises of more prosperous conditions. (Rival
powers, with aspirations and ideologies more or less similar to our
own, follow the same general course.)

Thus it becomes possible for the Administration and most
major American institutions to justify this country as the innocent object of world envy and hate, though we have no territorial designs and "want nothing for ourselves," though we fought
two great wars for justice and peace, though peace would be
impossible without our nuclear power and without our firmness
against "aggression" in Vietnam. We are infinitely more sinned
against than sinning, the panegyric goes, we who have given
most generously to poor nations, who have sent our youth abroad
to "help" them. Now we are beleaguered by Communist ob-

sessions with world domination and by the greed of all men. So the Rightist press would have it, so also most official rhetoric by former President Johnson or Dean Rusk.

At any rate, the net result is repression of the individual by society, a type of sublimated slavery. Most men believe what they need, it seems, and needs have been well defined and firmly implanted.

Technical progress and Communism, the plus and minus of control, are both pursued with clear purpose, sometimes with fanaticism. They are apparently enough to produce the profound cohesion and consensus which distinguish our society. Allow Madison Avenue to manipulate individual and group needs; keep the middle class and the rich content with preferential concern for business; silence the poor with periodic and overpublicized bits of social legislation—result, a welfare state. Seek foreign markets first by a colonial, and later by an imperialist, design; identify competitors as "enemies"; create an ideology to confront enemy "propaganda"; arm as a gesture of "defense"; keep hot- and cold-war situations various and turbulent—result, a warfare state. In operation and in effect the two are complements, halves of the same coin. One needs the other; one would suffer widespread, even violent, change without the other.

Together, they can mobilize men, institutions, and a nation, purge traditional trouble spots, eliminate historical grievances, smother opposition and dissent, keep a relative and ominous peace. Of its own kind, it is an astounding achievement, but under Christian judgment it is so destructive of human values that it is like a horror film shown too fast and enticingly to be understood.

The main dynamics and trends of producing conformity through socioeconomic processes are destructive enough to be delineated again. Mythologize national needs as being identical with big-business needs; encourage industrial cartels through numberless mergers; absorb labor into management by giving labor its demands, and sometimes more; provide capital with investment outlets through worldwide systems of economic and military pacts, monetary arrangements, and assistance programs; allow a free press that censors itself through devotion to national purpose; buy the ghetto off by "pacification" money in the hot summer and by allowing it to destroy itself at other times; use churches and synagogues to moralize the grandeur of a "free" society and the "integrity" of national interest, invade homes and classrooms with mass communications and with conformist public opinion; poll the public on key establishment concerns, then react to polls instead of human needs; standardize leisure and recreation as conditioners for contentment and happiness; assimilate leadership into business, government, and church; keep dossiers on trouble-makers, and keep them under discreet surveillance; employ military indoctrination as another species of thought-control, and entrust to the military abroad the same function given the police at home.

There is much more, if one intends to bore or stun a reader. But it should be made clear that such analysis is not part of a "hate America" campaign. Rather, it can be applied with slight variations to Great Britain, France, West Germany, Italy, even to the Soviet Union. In Russia direct political controls are being noticeably relaxed in favor of technological controls, the controls of an affluent society. In France and Italy two of the strongest Communist parties in the world choose to play parliamentarianism, not as a waiting game, but in direct admission of capitalist power to assimilate them and condemn them to the nonradical.

America, however, is far and away the pattern and outstanding example. The technological and cultural influences we export are received with mixed emotions in the most remote tribal villages, in the most antagonistic Communist countries. To paraphrase Herbert Marcuse, two antithetical propositions are now being clarified: (1) Technological society is capable of containing qualitative change indefinitely. (2) Technological society has within itself forces of violence which can tear it apart. We may never know which of the two wins out, for a third possibility may intrude, World War III.

To say that the Church is sharing man's crisis today is a gen-

erous claim, true only to a point. To state that the Church per-
ceives the nature of man's crisis, and enters it in faith and service,
is to risk absurdity. Such an observation, of course, is not meant
to demean millions of believers whose honest desire is to implant
Christ's kingdom and His justice in man's family. It is merely to
insist on their failure (and one's own) to do so.

Many Christians take heart from signs of Church renewal, and
they point with eagerness and relief to better qualities of training, liturgy, social sensitivity, service, authority, and *conscience*.
Openness to other Christians, to Jews, humanists, and unbelievers,
is a remarkable and encouraging commonplace. Christians are
even talking to Communists, and finding the experience full of
common concerns and anxieties.

One might venture, however, that such criteria of "progress"
miss the mark and even become delusions in themselves. It is of
little immediate purpose or ultimate consequence to reflect on
where we were and the distance we have traversed. Such reflections lead us to forget the fact that the Church is under judgment from both the Gospel and the world, and to neglect them
while concentrating on the energies and ingenuities expended in
"renewal" is a dangerous ingroup pastime.

The Gospel indicts us because we do not believe its words
and therefore cannot take it seriously. Part of that dilemma is
that we cannot imagine it "working," which is to say that there
is no point in practicing it until all men practice it. Since that
eventuality is unlikely, one is discharged from responsibility.
Arguments amassed to justify our version of Christianity even
become startling replicas of contemporary thinking; contradictory
propositions are the favorite tool of such reasonableness. So
Christians will say, "Defensive wars can be fought because the
gospel doesn't outlaw them." Or they will say, "Men are war-
like, war is inevitable, so we support war!" And Americans will
say, "Peace is war—both Vietnam and overkill prove it!"

The world indicts us because we have little concern for it,
little allegiance to its aspirations and interests, little time for its
plight. The world we fear and ostracize—containing the greater
portion of men—is one of hunger and suffering, one of awakening

consciousness, one of gathering bitterness and hate. It is a world whose cry is "revolution" and whose desire is to cast off its chains and destroy its guards, or to die trying. Ironically enough, it is a world that Christians are commanded to enter, whereas they are equally commanded to leave the world of privilege in which they live. And since they neither know this new world nor sympathize with its agony (having no intention of abandoning their privileges), there can be no reconciliation expected from them. How could there be? Presence and prophecy must precede reconciliation; but when these preliminaries are neglected, personal integrity in Christians becomes as unlikely as the just social order that flows from it.

More and more, people speak of revolution "within" this country, and though disagreements might arise about its causes and nature, few will deny its likelihood and threat. Granted, therefore, the probability of revolution, what course will it take? Nonviolent revolution is impossible without Christians; it is also impossible with Christians as they are. Violent revolution, then, becomes very nearly inevitable.

But we are attempting here to understand the Church in a technological society. One can begin such a discussion by theologizing about the Church as a community of faith and service; then one can speculate about a technocracy and the distinctive society it builds; and finally, one can judge how the two interact and influence one another. Nevertheless, our object will be to venture that a technocracy and a church are institutionally compatible, but that it is virtually impossible for an institutional church to be a Christian community under a technocracy.

It is a fact of existence that the Christian Church must live under worldly power; it is also a fact that it lives at peace with this power more often than not. Power in the United States (the epitome of Western capitalist technocracy) is an institutional triumvirate: the military, economic, and political bureaucracies. Political design, whether domestic or foreign, stems from these three bureaucracies which in turn stem from a mass-production, mass-consumer society that now welcomes war-making as an integral operation. Which is to say that our free-enterprise technocracy has now overproduced for its domestic and foreign markets, and consequently must have war-making as a new market, as an imperial protection for foreign markets, and as a safety valve for its inherent violence. It seems safe to conjecture, therefore, that war-making is here to stay for the immediate future, because our capitalism simply cannot discard it as a rising portion of the gross national product.

To put it differently, war-making carries the built-in waste-making of mass consumerism to an ultimate logic. Planned obsolescence in autos, appliances, and buildings makes more rational (or irrational) the combat waste of war material and the phasing-out of this material for faster and more deadly equipment. Add to this our assault upon space, and its connection with arms research and development.

In addition, war-making as a quasi-marketable function gives credence to our ambition to conduct the world's business: It intimidates the poor, pressures them to become and/or remain our customers, sobers their rage and unrest. If war-making fails in this regard, we have a Vietnam; if it succeeds, we have counter-insurgency, teamed with political scientists and their conflict-management. Whatever the case, however, war-making is a profitable item of the economy, a factor of planned waste, an investment that pays for itself in rising prosperity and foreign profits.

This triumvirate of military, economic, and political bureaucracies runs America. In spite of disclaimers, moreover, its policy and operation make clear its intention to run the world. It is a coalition that is interdependent and interlocking, as sensitive to reciprocal needs as it is jealous of its power. Its weaknesses baffle its friends and enrage its critics; its aims affect hundreds of millions; its excesses frighten men everywhere. It is a coalition imperial in design and ambition, arrogant, ruthless, cohesive in organization, and awesome in military might. It is instrumental in making America what is perhaps the last of history's many empires.

The Church should be the adversary of this dizzying concentration of power, yet it is not. The Church should be challenging its moral relativism, its anticommunism and antirevolutionary ideology, its imperial economics, ambiguous racism, hot and cold warring, its mounting control over a passive and neurotic citizenry, its thing-obsession and people-domination. The Church should understand that this idolatry is engaged in a fearful race between violence-production and violence-management, that it is now an obstacle to human progress and a threat to mankind. And yet it does not understand, does not challenge.

To expect it to understand, to challenge, to become an adversary of such massive and coordinated injustice is perhaps to expect too much. It is perhaps to lay too great a public burden upon the Church. Perhaps. But where do allegiances lie, except to Christ and to man? And where does hope lie? If the Church does not withstand power's authority to plunge deeper into the doomsday race, to escalate further the insanity in Vietnam, to suck excessive profits from the Third World, to allow our cities to verge on explosion, what moral authority does the Church possess? If these crimes are not immoral, what is morality? If the Church does not assert that the overlords of this nation have clearly lost the right to public jurisdiction over Americans in many areas of policy dealing with war, race, and war taxes, what is the substance of its gospel? If the Church judges divorces, uncelibate priests, couples practicing birth control, clerical revolutionaries, and Marxists as morally irresponsible, why should it not judge those who make, administer, and profit from war as criminally irresponsible? Obviously, the War Crimes Tribunals, called twice at Stockholm and Copenhagen, should have been sponsored jointly by the Vatican and the World Council of Churches.

Christians should have refused to send their young men to war, refused to pay war taxes, and refused to work in defense industries. Christians should have led draft protestors into jail, with bishops and Head Clerks in the vanguard. Christians should have disrupted military bases nonviolently; they should have, with total respect for conscience, encouraged refusal of Vietnam service and even desertion from the military. Christians should have attempted to close down war production and to destroy war machinery as a means of protecting the lives of those who operate it. Christians should have synthesized an economics that would save their countrymen from becoming the commercial rapists of the world. In a word, Christians should have fought with the weapons of their witness to make this nation honest, to force conformity with its Declaration of Independence, its commitment to the United Nations Charter, its rhetoric about self-determination. But because they have not, honest men deride the Church or courteously ignore it while, more dangerously still, the masters of society favor and commend it.

Assuredly, such acts would be a public burden upon the Church. But what of its gospel and calling? Because it has adulterated both to shameful degrees, it has helped to push America to the brink of violent revolution, and it has helped to set the world aflame. In point of fact, Christian hypocrisy has helped to stage a scenario of tragic dimensions, a whirlwind that mankind is just beginning to reap. Which says something about the price that will be paid for Christian wealth, comfort, and arrogance.

It may now be apparent that certain factors intervene to make the Church an ally of power bureaucrats instead of, given the need, their moral critic and adversary. Apart from certain historical-religious influences that have shaped American Christianity, it may be far more important to stress the impact of bureaucracy upon the Church. One can give endless attention to these influences: the Puritan ethic, the Calvinist impact on economics, missionary efforts at home and abroad (parallels to economic expansionism), denominational differences and similarities, the Catholic assimilation of immigrants, the "separation" of Church and State, patriotism as an ethical tax. But in measure of influence, much of the above has been superseded by Christian unanimity favoring institutionalism—what critics call the bureaucracy of moralism.

By way of style and operation, bureaucracies tend to concentrate on indigenous purposes and objectives. In a general manner, therefore, business focuses on profits; government legislates local, national, and international commonweal (American

economic health); defense protects our freedom (American economic freedom); education gives people marketable skills; church
lends to all its weight of moral approval. In a very real sense
their value system is the same and their language similar, as is
their allegiance for administration and their appreciation of power.
And at their summit are the men who run and rule the country,
the men whom C. Wright Mills called "The Power Elite."

Since bureaucracies share a common power base—citizen, busi-
nessman, ex-serviceman, Christian—and since this power base provides a common point of departure into specific enterprises,
harmony becomes an operational necessity and dialogue a necessary tool. Bureaucrats therefore think it essential to know the main
interests and directions of other bureaucrats, and this they accomplish by maintaining an active presence within several key
bureaucracies. A case in point would be the local tie-ins between
manufacturing, sales, news media, finance, law, insurance, and
church. One man can be an insurance executive, sit on the board
of a bank, hold stock in local TV, and be on the vestry of his
church or serve as an adviser to his bishop. Meanwhile, he remains active in the Rotary or the Chamber of Commerce, eats
lunch and drinks cocktails with his peers.

Expand such allegiances to a national level, and one has a
coalition of military, industrial, and political interests that have
instant and easy access to one another, simply because the coalition's members understand that their personal and bureaucratic
viability depends upon the oil in a wider machinery. Such men
have transcendent loyalties, and these are not to God.

What results is a symbiotic relationship. Bureaucratic purposes
are harmonized, streamlined, and widened; the links between them
are firmed and strengthened. The product is a force of single-
minded purpose, complex efficiency, and massive power—grudging
of freedom, lavish in reward, ruthless to outside threat.

A Christian can allow much more entrenchment in secular institutions than in his church, since he knows that their different
covenants ought to foster different types of power. He knows
that historically, industrialization helped to make bureaucracies

inevitable, even as technology now makes them larger and more complex. But he also knows that his church is a community, not a bureaucracy; that it is in fact very nearly a community *against* a bureaucracy. Obviously, it may institutionalize, but when that choice makes the Gospel an ersatz code, a Christian institution has become bureaucracy. In effect it has lost its freedom to be Christian—and human.

When that happens, the Church speaks the language of official-dom, the ethical equivalent of propaganda. It moralizes in a casuistic, neutral fashion, betraying where, in fact, its values lie. And they lie with its own bureaucracy, with its contributing members and its public image, with the tolerant credence it can arouse in other circles of power. The dynamics of its system lead it to the assumption that survival and growth require neutrality toward injustice, and once the assumption is accepted, neutrality becomes a price quite eagerly paid.

Which is to say that the Church responds with what the secular establishment asks: with a caliber of speech which clothes the atrocities of power in white garments of probity, which obscures the violence of technological materialism, which offers a superstitious palliative to the fierce tensions of technological life, and which makes one form of unreality more liveable by substituting another. The message has little to do with real life but much to do with support of life as it is led. It substitutes confidence in power for faith, or it helps to make the two one.

The public position of religious bureaucracy follows its speech consistently. If honest speech is to be shunned, so too is honest witness. In frequent contrast, secular power may conclude that a "liberal" position on human rights is to its interest. But this is not necessarily true of the Church, whose response is first to its institutional base—making it more inbred than social, more operational than ordained to a larger service of men. On the other hand, both government and business must sometimes be sensitive to their constituency and market—survival and sales sometimes demand a kind of group-interest altruism.

If Vietnam became a gut issue by endangering the Church's

bureaucracy, the present neutrality would dissolve. Bishops would become doves, chanceries would sponsor draft counseling and would house deserters, clerics would minister to prisoners from within jails. But since little prospect of such a threat exists, since the war does not affect the Church's property, income, investments, membership, or privileges to any noticeable degree, silence and inaction become (and remain) policy. Given these realities, it is indeed possible to imagine the Church doing business as usual while 1984 or the first nuclear exchange is upon us.

By the same token, urban turmoil is not seen by the Church's bureaucratic vision as directly "its" issue. Church members live outside the ghetto for the most part, and those who do concern themselves with urban problems do not seriously negate the rule. The value system, dynamics, and machinery of the Church are not primarily directed toward blacks. If one were to except their motivation for a moment, both the Government and business exhibit far more honest concern in the Riot Commission Report (March, 1968) or in employment efforts than does the Church.

Briefly, the similarity of view and action between church and secular bureaucracies is brought about not so much because there is a moral vacuum created by the Church and exploited by the Government (though there is some truth in that), or because Washington must load its propaganda with moralism to advance credibility (some truth in that also), but because bureaucracies are at heart the same, and they are the same because a harmony or an interdependence of interest prevails between them. In a largely unconscious and unarticulated display of mutual concern, both the Church and the State promote the national purpose. And if their visceral reasons for doing so vary, the net result is substantially the same.

Let no one be surprised, therefore, that in exchange for being left alone by the Church in political and commercial "overreach" like nuclear-arms escalation, "rollback" foreign policy, Vietnam, the CIA, and economic invasions of both developed and developing countries, Washington grants immunities and privileges to the Church—tax exemptions, clerical dispensations from military service, grants for education and research, and consistent official approval. There is no overt contract for such mutual back-scratch-ing, but there is a covenant lying soddenly in the guts of bureauc-racies, a covenant to which all spouses are blasphemously faithful.

The covenant between bureaucracies indicates, by and large, their response to one another. The Church responds much as it is expected to, at least on leadership levels. Officially, it does let the Government alone, thereby giving huge tacit support as well—and on occasion, enthusiastic affirmation—to domestic and foreign policy. Herein lies its tragedy and the price of its betrayal. It gives support to power at the expense of conscience. Many of its mem-bers would be more Christian without it.

What is the future of religious bureaucracy? It is difficult and sobering to say. Bureaucracy can feel little urgency for change, nor can it accuse itself of massive complicity in America's crimes. But this much seems somewhat clear. It is breaking up—ponder-ously, incredulously—all forms of Christian and Jewish adherence. The fresh air that Pope John let into the Catholic Church is now blowing through the whole believing world, scattering before it the religious trash of centuries, leaving the faithful less and less to work with except man and his agony.

As long as retrenchment goes on, as long as renewal means only better housekeeping, as long as justice is neither spoken nor lived, the base of the religious establishment will erode like the feet of a huge clay god. Honest people will go their way and pursue their consciences, much as though church and synagogue did not exist. Clergymen will reject authoritarianism, middle-class dishonesty, and social irrelevance to leave the ministry. The best of the young, meanwhile, will hunt for substitutes, refusing affiliation with a structure so impervious to change, so immune to suffering, so con-tradictory to itself.

And this is a hopeful trend, because from it will come new Christian communities, small, poor by choice, passionate for jus-tice, revolutionary, losing themselves among the victims of man's greed. They will be, above all, communities of the Spirit, Who calls to them whom He will, that the redemption of Christ might go on in a world torn by movements of hope and catastrophe.

"This day I set you over nations and over kingdoms, to root up

and tear down, to destroy and to demolish, to build and to plant"
(Jeremias 1:10). "I am the true vine, and my Father is the vine-
dresser. Every branch in me that bears no fruit he will take away;
and every branch that bears fruit he will cleanse, that it may bear
more fruit" (John 15:1-2). "Must then a Christ perish in torment
in every age, to save those who have no imagination?" (Epilogue
to George Bernard Shaw's *St. Joan*).

II

The Color of Poverty

∾∾∾∾∾∾∾∾∾∾∾∾∾∾∾∾∾∾∾∾∾∾∾∾∾∾∾∾∾∾∾∾∾∾∾

Old Maggie's sweat would drip and sizzle
on that cast iron range she stoked
but she was grinding at the handle
of our great big ice cream freezer
that day she had her stroke.
It put a damper on my mother's luncheon.
All the ladies in their picture hats and organdies
hushed up until the ambulance took Maggie off
but soon I heard
their shrieks of laughter
like the bird-house at the zoo
while they spooned in
their fresh peach cream.
  —JOHN BEECHER, from *To Live and Die in Dixie*

SOMEBODY ONCE SAID THAT WHITE AMERICA
doesn't really want to be what it is and doesn't really want what it
has. The observation is a safe one, capable of application to any

person, majority group, or nation. In the most irrepressible fashion, people desire to be more rather than to be less, desire quality over quantity. Whatever their condition of life, people insist on hope, and being better is substantially the realization of hope.

Nonetheless, the observation is not exactly to the point. However much whites in America might long for a quality of life flowing from human relationships with blacks, however much they might desire peace in their possessions through sharing them with others, society intrudes itself into the deliberations to oppose them and to help smother and still them.

Significantly, some polls on race relations show that certain whites feel guilty about their relationships with blacks, feel that justice has not been done black people, and that America is in for serious trouble until more justice becomes a fact. "Granted!" one is inclined to answer—"events seem to prove them out." From that point of realization, however, the way to justice becomes very murky; and meantime, guilt is not dispelled, justice is not done black folk, and serious trouble does come. Something has intervened to nullify good will, to deepen guilt, and to cause even an increased intransigence. There's a hang-up, as they say.

The hang-up is that on the one hand, whites are immersed in the values of a society that exists almost solely for their benefit, and on the other, they are tortured by America's myth of equality and by its precise application to black people. The two cannot jell, so to speak; one or the other has to change. And since black people will not hear of any change of the latter but will rather insist that the myth become actuality, society must change. To that, whites say in all practicality that society cannot change: "We run it, and it's for us, and therefore black people will have to change"—that is, remain silent.

The real conversion that whites must therefore undergo to accord justice to blacks amounts of necessity to a kind of rebellion and running war against nearly everything America is. Whites have too much to lose by such a process, however, and so even the best of us content ourselves with rhetoric or half measures. In contrast, blacks have nothing to lose and can be increasingly expected to attempt to destroy a society they cannot share.

It is both true and untrue that a welfare-warfare state like America (a consumer society in constant imperialist expansion under the cover of weaponry) must have its victims. It is true, because the welfare-warfare state could not remain precisely that if it did not have its victims. It is untrue, because it would not have any victims if it was willing to reform its conscience to find more human avenues for the use of the genius of laboratory and technology in city planning, adequate income, improved education and housing, the purification of air and water. A new conscience must, however, attack our obsessive attachment to goods, to the profit motivation, and to the rights of property which seemingly secure goods. And this amounts to taking back part of what has already been maintained—the very definition of a welfare-warfare state.

At the present time American technocracy's victims are the black man and the poor man, who number nearly one quarter of the population. One could further complicate the issue by offering the hypothesis that the middle class and the rich are victimized most of all. But within the limits of discussion, the exploitation of the poor and of colored people becomes more possible in an industrial society because machines tend to mechanize humans; that is to say, machines tend to subject those who run or use them to their own style, rhythm, and product. The mechanical stamp on personality and character helps to malform a man by giving him an affinity to things, which in their unchangeable character and service make him secure and confident.

Such a profound influence overlaps inevitably into human areas, and in such a way that other people are often dealt with by "thing" judgment: They must exhibit the predictability of things or else be rejected. Human relationships are therefore entered into with fear and insecurity, since a gnawing sense tells one that people are not things, that they are capable of reaches of good and evil beyond familiar patterns, that they can be the cause of bewilderment and anxiety. "Things" are not that way; rather, they deepen the fantasy that life is doing a job or not doing it, that the world is Manichaean, and that force alone can control that which is not understood.

Blend such liabilities with a historical racism as fiercely in-grained as any in history, and one has cause enough for our terri-ble predicament in race relations. Nowhere in the world is a social problem so scrutinized by social scientists, theologians and politi-cians; nowhere, too, are conclusions so impaired by imperception, arrogance, and politicizing. The enormous goodwill and energy which Americans vigorously bring to an issue are here largely nul-lified by mysterious factors not understood, much less dealt with.

The net result, in spite of considerable study, work, and expense, is apt to be projects understaffed and underfunded, top-heavy, fumbling, and self-defeating. It has been said: Bring Americans to any technical problem in the world, and if it can be solved, it will be; bring them to any collective human problem, and they are liable to entrench it or to make it worse.

It is not so much that we fail to see race relations as a human, moral problem; it is that we cannot deal as people with human relationships. Reductively, then, black people in general or a movement like black nationalism or a political ambition like Black Power is telling us that we are inhuman, since we cannot deal justly with others not of our own stamp, and that they will not wait until we can. Integration of the races is not the point; neither is racial separatism. The point is one that black people make: What means are available to a black community universally re-jected by whites who, despite guilt and unsophisticated goodwill, are incapable of living justly with other people?

National reactions each summer follow an exact historical course often repeated since 1954. A majority of whites, with desperate good intention, call for more and better programs in the ghetto; others demand the suppression of "lawlessness." Blacks increasingly reject both approaches—that of the first because ghetto programs never receive enough funds to suggest either seriousness or sincerity and are therefore patronizing and clearly an effort to pacify blacks with maximum economy. Blacks reject the second because it is impossible without the universal suspen-sion of black rights. And this, America is not willing to do, at least presently.

Race relations are further complicated by America's penchant for war. By every evidence this country is fairly content to shift its treasure from domestic needs into a ridiculous and vicious Southeast Asian war, bringing to light real attitudes and values in American personal and institutional life. These attitudes whites will refuse to admit, although they expend considerable time defending them with rationalizations. Consequently, America's police action in Vietnam both protects the exploitative system that oppresses blacks and also allows Negro ghettos to rot, ferment, and *pay*. That is why Stokely Carmichael is precise in saying that Vietnam is a racist war: Vietnamese are brown people who are being decimated by military intervention despite our protestations to the contrary; and blacks pay proportionately more in blood and taxes for Vietnam than whites do.

Few prospects seem possible save ghetto rumblings and eruptions, which could chain-react across the face of the land, so provoking whites that they will impose a massive policy of containment to put down the uprising. Such a future is not to be wondered at; it is indeed a logical consequence to the fear with which blacks are regarded and to the violence to which they are subjected. One must see that blacks are tolerated only so long as they are quiet, tractable, and "nonviolent." When they are not, when they register militancy and riot, traditional forms of violence must be proportionately increased until the blacks are once more forced to slip back into their "place."

Situations are up for export, they say, just like goods and guns. Our hatred of blacks, disgust with the poor, terror of Communists, suppression of the ghetto, and the policies by which we handle such contingencies are now up for export and are being routed around the globe. The cold war has undergone drastic change; it is no longer East-West, but North-South; no longer ideological, but racial; no longer cold, but hot. It is not necessary to predict these horrors; their ominous reality is already upon us. And they are apt to swell under their own momentum, since one can notice little countervailing analysis or movement in America or in the West.

Yet one must try to understand the struggle and to see it in the light of one's Christianity and solidarity with mankind. Understanding, moreover, will illumine a fact over which Christians should rejoice: Injustice in the world is no longer ignored, endured, or tolerated. It is protested, and redress is made in reasonable time, or injustice is paid back in similar coin. Understanding also includes a sense of the history of American racism and how it now contributes to racial separatism of world proportions.

One of the fabrications that whites in America employ (or whites elsewhere, depending on the degree of black presence) is the peculiarly distorted and unscholarly argument that blacks are labeled for inferiority by color and made thereby a lesser type of human species. Such mythology is the basis for justifying injustice toward blacks and whatever intensity injustice takes, from violent discrimination to smug paternalism. Myth becomes conviction, conviction becomes pathology, and pathology was at the root of slavery and the brutal repression of the Reconstruction period, which gave way grudgingly before manpower and military needs in two great wars and before black militancy in the Civil Rights Era.

Racial pathology still inspires us to regard blacks as national liabilities and perpetual welfare clients who ought to proceed to white patrons with ingenuous affability, with hands extended, with "a mountain of yesses and grins," as John Howard Griffin puts it. Racial pathology causes us to regard the black man as a parasite upon the national body, as the embodiment of cultural gap, as a test of our magnanimity, as someone we are unhappily stuck with, since a return to slavery or to Africa is out of the question. It may therefore dispel part of this tragic mental darkness if we dwell upon the black contribution to this country, so that we might better recognize our black brothers as early immigrants, as stalwart soldiers, as pioneers in the East, South, and West, as journeymen in field, shop, and factory, as citizens no less in slavery than in segregation, as the brunt of white crimes and the carrier of white burdens, as innovators of protest and nonviolent resistance, as the hope to Christianity, as friends and brothers.

It may startle some of us to know that twenty blacks arrived at Jamestown, Virginia, in August of 1619, a year before the *May-*

flower landed at Plymouth and 244 years before the signing of the Emancipation Proclamation. Their presence here infused new life into the European slave trade, which had been going on for nearly two hundred years and which continued for more than two hundred years. Nothing is more callous than trafficking in human beings, but imagination is stimulated to horror by the fact that in four hundred years Africa was raped of forty millions of its people, roughly half of which came to America. Millions more died before and after capture while being taken to ship or on board. At any rate, the advent of the first twenty began the greatest forced migration in human history, the sorriest chapter in the annals of our nation, and what could be justly termed as the most valuable contribution of one continent to another, one people to another, one race to another.

It is important nonetheless to remember that the original twenty blacks were not slaves but indentured servants who found themselves in an established socioeconomic system expressing no connotations of racial inferiority. They joined company with paupers, religious dissenters, orphans, prisoners, and prostitutes, who like themselves discharged their servitude, earned their freedom, and mingled with the other settlers on a strict basis of equality.

This relatively happy state, however, could not last for the first blacks and for those who followed them. White greed saw to that. Virginia and Maryland took the initiative among the colonies by imposing slavery in the 1660's, and it was not long before color became a badge of servitude in all the colonies, stripping blacks of all human rights. Poor whites and Indians who shared indenture with blacks had the protection of government and tribe and could easily escape; in contrast, blacks had no protective government, no recourse to law, were too visible to hide or escape, and as the Spanish used to say, were worth four times their number of Indians. At first, the Bible became the rationalization for slavery; being unbaptized, a black had no status. Or slavery was imposed as a blessing, because a slave could be baptized and made Christian. Later, color became the rationale, and the Bible was employed as the authority for inferiority and complete servitude. In any real sense, however, economics stood as the conviction behind slavery—blacks were helpless, strong, adaptable, and hence, valuable.

So it was that slavery laid its cursed hold upon the land. By 1710 there were 50,000 black slaves in America; when the Declaration of Independence was signed, there were 500,000; when the Civil War broke out, there were over 4,000,000.

Eric Williams writes:

The Western World is in danger of forgetting today what the Negro has contributed to Western civilization. . . . London and Bristol, Bordeaux and Marseilles, Cadiz and Seville, Lisbon and New England, all waxed fat on the profits of the trade in the tropical produce raised by the Negro slave. Capitalism in England, France, Holland and colonial America received a double stimulation—from the manufacture of goods needed to exchange for slaves, woolen and cotton goods, copper and brass vessels, and the firearms, handcuffs, chains and torture instruments indispensable on the slave ships and on the slave plantation.

He rather fatuously continues:

This contribution of the Negro has failed to receive adequate recognition. It is more than ever necessary to remember it today. England and France, Holland, Spain and Denmark, not to mention the United States, Brazil and other parts of South America are all indebted to Negro labor.[1]

W. E. B. DuBois took a different tack, and ignoring what black people have given to this country, concerned himself with what it cost to give it:

Raphael painted, Luther preached, Corneille wrote, and Milton sang; and through it all, for four hundred years, the dark captives wound to the sea amid the bleaching bones of the dead; for four hundred years the sharks followed the scurrying ships; for four hundred years America was strewn with the living and dying millions of a transplanted race; for four hundred years Ethiopia stretched forth her hands unto God.[2]

Ironically enough, black men fought in the American Revolution for the freedom of their masters, a freedom nonetheless denied them. Harriet Beecher Stowe observed this in wonderment:

It was not for their own land they fought, not even for a land which had adopted them, but for a land which had enslaved them, and whose laws, even in freedom, oftener oppressed than protected. Bravery, under such circumstances, has a peculiar beauty and merit.[3] **1486315**

Crispus Attucks, a black freedman, was one of the first men killed in the Boston Massacre; the two Salems, Peter Salem and Salem Poor, were among the most valiant soldiers of the war. Before the Revolution ended, some five thousand blacks, both slaves and freedmen, had taken up arms to defend a liberty that could not be theirs. Moreover, Europeans were not the only foreigners to respond to America's call for help. School children are taught that Kosciuszko and Lafayette came, but not many Americans know that Haiti sent its Fontages Legion, which helped to save the revolutionary cause at the seige of Savannah.

The Revolutionary War helped to free forces that worked to eliminate strict slavery in the North. But the war had little effect upon the South, where a ruthless decision had been made to use blacks as flesh-and-blood props to economy, custom, and the Southern "Way of Life." Aspects of introverted aristocracy, demented folk culture, and economic totalitarianism have also been used to describe a society built upon black backs. Historians of the period tell us that for two hundred years a social structure as coercive as any yet known was built upon the most implacable racial prejudice known in any land or age. The Negro historian Lerone Bennett calls it, with great accuracy, the "Cotton Curtain."

Individual, family, and collective rights were totally and arbitrarily stripped away; dehumanization became a system and an institution. It became a crime to teach blacks how to read and write, a crime even to give them a Bible. According to usual practice, families were not allowed to exist as families, children were sold away from their mothers, and fatherhood was deprived of any legal standing. The rape of a slave woman was ruled by a Mississippi court to be outside the range of common or civil law. "The father of a slave," said a Kentucky court, "is unknown to our law."

Children were often herded to the fields at six and seven years. Women were valued by their masters as much for breeding qualities as for the ability to perform field drudgery under a burning

sun. Seldom did a slave live out his life without a flogging of
thirty-nine to one hundred lashes from a cowhide whip, and it
was not infrequent that sadistic masters would flog the skin from
a back and then wash down the back in brine.

Toil in the fields under a driver, overseer, and master was long
unremitting, and harsh. Ten or fifteen minutes were allowed at
noon for a crust and a lump of bacon, then they went back to
work until dark. Later at the slave compound wood had to be cut,
mules and swine fed. Only then could supper be cooked and eaten
without simple amenities like knives, forks, and plates. "Slavery
time was tough, boss," said one ex-slave; "you just don't know how
tough it was." It should shock us not at all to hear a historian like
Stanley M. Elkins comment that the only "mass experience that
Western people have had within recorded history comparable in
any way with Negro slavery was undergone in the nether world
of Nazism. The concentration camp was not only a perverted
slave system; it was also—what is less obvious but even more to
the point—a perverted patriarchy."[4]

Yet American black people endured under slavery; they sur-
vived and did more than that. They waxed strong through a simple, uncomplicated fight for existence. Alternatives were clear and
utterly real: Either develop qualities of soul which transformed
oppression into life, or die. They chose to live, in departure from
brown and red men of other places and other climates who drank
the white man's whiskey, read his Bible, diminished under his
work, and wasted away into extinction. Slaves drank the white
man's whiskey, read his Bible, did his work, and flourished. Undoubtedly, this decision to live is at once the strength and the
glory of black men, nor is it one to be underestimated or forgotten
today. Their decision for life founded the wealth of this country,
which rested, as Lincoln believed, "on the 250 years of unrequited
toil of Negro men and women." Frederick Douglass, the great
Negro abolitionist, spoke of this decision to live and of the stake
in America that black men gained in result:

We are here, and here are we likely to be. To imagine that we shall
ever be eradicated is absurd and ridiculous. We can be remodified,

changed and assimilated, but never extinguished. We repeat, therefore, that we are here, and that this is our country. . . . We shall neither die out, nor be driven out; but shall go with this people, either as a testimony against them, or as evidence in their favor throughout their generations.[5]

The Negro contribution did not end with revolutionary service and the terrible sacrifices of slavery. The Negro's efforts to preserve the Union that had so abused him were of equal significance. Outside Richmond, in 1864, a black division swept away entrenched Confederate opposition, suffered bloody losses, and won for thirteen men the Congressional Medal of Honor. To most of them the medal was awarded posthumously.

To be sure, the willingness of black men to fight, and their capability to do so, long preceded the indecisiveness of Lincoln and the Federal Government to use Negro troops, since policy tended to look upon the Civil War as a white man's war, with the attendant implication that it was slightly "immoral" to enlist those over whom the war was being fought. Men like Union Generals Benjamin Butler, John Lane, and David Hunter, however, unofficially organized black regiments and brigades. At one point, in 1863, Butler heard of 1,400 free Louisiana blacks who themselves had organized a regiment. He sent for their leaders and asked if they would fight. Their answer was classic. "General," their spokesman said, "we come of a fighting race. Our fathers were brought here because they were captured in war, and in hand to hand fights, too. We are willing to fight. Pardon me, General, but the only cowardly blood we have got in our veins is the white blood."[6]

And so they fought. Acceptance in the Union Army was tenuous; attitudes toward them ranged from contempt to mere toleration. Pay was often half what white soldiers received; state legislatures consistently reneged on paying black troops a private's pay of thirteen dollars a month. Moreover, capture by the Confederates meant murder, or if one were lucky, mere torture and a return to slavery. Yet in spite of all, fifty thousand black soldiers were serving the Union cause by the end of 1863, and in key engagements at Port Hudson, Milliken's Bend, Fort Wagner,

Poison Spring, Olustee, Nashville, Petersburg, and over four
hundred other places, they hurried the end of America's bloodiest
war.

There is, perhaps, no need to give an exhaustive history of the
black response to this country in the face of constant mistreat-
ment, brutality, terror, and death. Patterns were set very early,
and show an unvarying consistency through American history, displaying on the one hand what blacks have received from this
country, and what in turn they have given. Reference can be
made, for example, to what has been termed the Terrible Nineties,
the 1890's, when a black man was lynched every two days or so—
not for alleged rape, which was seldom, but for other crimes, like
testifying against a white man in court, seeking other employment,
failing to use "Mister" to whites, arguing over the price of black-
berries (a classic case), attempting to vote, accepting a job as
postmaster, or just being too prosperous.

Lerone Bennett sums up the pitiable and inhuman spectacle of
those days in this fashion:

To work from sun up to sun down for a whole year and to end owing
"the man" $400 for the privilege of working; to do this year after year
and to sink deeper and deeper into debt; to be chained to the land by
bills at the plantation store; to wash away this knowledge with bad gin,
to blot it out in an ecstasy of song and prayer; to sing, to pray, to cry;
to bring forth a boy child and to be told one night that four thousand
people are roasting him slowly over a hot fire and leisurely cutting off
his fingers and toes; to be powerless and to curse one's self for cowardice; to be conditioned by dirt and fear and shame and signs; to become a part of these signs and to feel them in the deepest recess of the
spirit; to be knocked down in the streets and whipped for not calling a
shiftless hillbilly "Mister"; to be a plaything of judges and courts and
policemen; to be black in a white fire and to believe finally in one's own
unworthiness; to be without books and words and pretty pictures; to be
without newspapers and radios; to be without *understanding* . . . ; to
not know why it is happening; . . . to not know where to go and what
to do to stay the whip and the rope and the chain; to give in finally; to
bow, to scrape, to grin; and to hate one's self for one's servility and
weakness and blackness—all this was a Kafkaian nightmare which continued for days and nights and years.[7]

Nevertheless, out of this has come an infusion into the American scene as paradoxical as it is intense, one that has frightened whites because it has never really been understood. It is something far more essential and priceless than toil or valor in arms or monumental hardihood. Black gifts to America have been gifts of the spirit, gifts of the Cross. In his *Mind of the South* W. J. Cash puzzles over what he calls the "tyranny" that blacks hold over the customs and manners of white Southerners, and he wonders at the resilience of lives that can, under slavery and under a mockery of citizenship, influence others as strongly as they are influenced. When Carl Jung visited America, he immediately noticed the black imprint upon the psychology of the nation. "The first thing which attracted my attention," he remarked, "was the influence of the Negro, an obviously psychological difference regardless of any mixture of blood." Jung saw this influence apparent in the walking, singing, dancing, and even the praying, of white Americans.

Beyond that, and even more importantly, black men have been, even under slavery, the only Americans who have constantly made an issue of democracy. Their presence, protest, and appeal to *right* have forced this country to rewrite its Constitution and to rethink what has been so scandalously called the American dream of equality. Wherever they are found in this country, and whatever they do, black people indict the individual and national conscience, since white reactions to their presence inevitably bring to the surface attitudes of hypocrisy, cowardice, and personal slavery, giving at least faint hope that we will begin to understand that our personal images are largely myths and our personal accomplishments largely worthless. Black people presently supply the only example of heroism under oppression that this nation can claim, and whether the means be nonviolence or arson, the message is that revolution is not dead in America. Black people have so assaulted the ears and sensibilities of white Americans with cries for human rights and human dignity that the whole country has been dragged kicking and screaming into the debate—and were it not for the black revolution, it is hard to see how Jews, Puerto Ricans, migrant workers, and poor whites would now be faring as well as they are. Black people have insisted that human rights are either universal or nonexistent, and Stokely Carmichael's assertion that the draft "is white people sending black people to make war on yellow people in order to defend the land they stole from red people is precise, if unpopular.

Black people have shamed the churches for their lip service to the Gospel; it is no fantasy to say that Christians will be progressively forced to practice a true Christianity or to give it up entirely. Black people have been, moreover, the voice of justice and freedom which the Christian Church should have been but has not, and they know, with all the convictions of being black, that once they cease to be the moral voice of the nation, once they cease their moral belaboring of government, business, and labor, the Church is apt to settle again into the sanctuary, there to plan a better form of worship—or to dream of the next building project— while the country at large slides regressively into somnolence and barbarism, into childish, idle, and vicious pursuits. Black people have done more for ecumenism in the United States than any other force, and they have, in an odd way, collaborated with Pope John XXIII in helping us to understand that people are not to be feared and hated but loved, and that as soon as blacks are respected as persons, other hobgoblins will tend to disappear in favor of human beings, even though these be Communists, freethinkers, and hippies. Black people have shaken the governmental, economic, and social bureaucracy of this country, forcing it to look at itself, forcing it to lengths of understanding and response which otherwise would have been impossible, forcing it to the sullen and stubborn realization that as things stand now, the power structure has neither sympathy, room, nor provision for any people save whites, and that this condition cannot abide. Black men, finally, have written the death notices for white men. It is true, as Lerone Bennett notes, that blacks have been assisted by Auschwitz and Buchenwald, by Dresden, Hiroshima, and Nagasaki, even as they are assisted by Vietnam today. But the local obituaries have, nonetheless, come from Montgomery, Birmingham, Selma, Newark, and Detroit.

Nearly one hundred years ago Nietzsche said that God was dead in the hearts of his contemporaries. And now it is true to say that the white man is dead as a personification of superiority and selected mission, dead as one with an assumed mandate from God to coerce and limit men of darker skin, dead as one who considered himself the ruler of the earth, the heir of its wealth, the custodian of its destiny. The color of mankind has indeed changed, and for whites this means a terrifying freedom, since it invites us to break free of our foul and unhappy enclosure of mind, an enclosure whose walls are our fears, delusions, and myths, and whose anxious interior is proof enough of our fragility, limitation, and dependence.

One cannot shrug a shoulder at the past, for the past is part of the present and the future. America's racist dilemma is now the dilemma of the white West, that beleaguered minority of the world's peoples which stands guard over the earth's riches and protests with diminishing credibility its innocence and goodwill. Are Newark and Detroit the beginning of a serious reckoning? When will the whites of South Africa have their turn, or the Portuguese in Angola and Mozambique? Or, for that matter, the British, French, and Russians? For colonialism on the part of the white powers has not ceased; it has merely taken a subtle new form less and less tolerable to the colored poor of the world. It is the old issue of irresistible force and immovable object, and in the context of white-colored relationships it is likely to spell race war.

There are many ways to do violence to a man. Most of the Commandments prohibit interpersonal violence, and so we say a man should not harm his brother—should not injure him, take his property, steal his wife, ruin his name. He has rights, we say, and his rights are a living part of him—you harm him, you harm his rights; destroy him, destroy his rights. His rights are him in the abstract, we say, or at least they represent his value. And rights must dominate a relationship if it is to be just. Furthermore, we treat a man justly because we love him, and if he needs more from us than his rights seem to prompt, we love him more. Or so we say.

Obviously, racial relations become tragic if such convictions are professed rather than lived. They are also tragic if convictions are

professed and lived in a vacuum, with no hope or intention of
eliminating racism by what one believes and does. But racial relations are most tragic if convictions are not lived because one does
not believe that living them will eliminate racism one whit. In this
case convictions are abandoned because no immediate public result is seen. Living them does not "work," so why live them?

This is perhaps one of the more subtle dilemmas of whites
vis-à-vis blacks, a dilemma of not doing what is right for the
wrong reasons (which is not to imply that there are right reasons
for not doing right). The wrong reasons in this instance include
an ignorance of black history, an unawareness of how Americans
institutionalize racism, an incomprehension of how a technological
society militates against social justice. The wrong reasons must
also include a refusal to admit that whites take in racism with their
mothers' milk, that they breathe it from an institutional atmosphere, that their folklore and mythology are white supremacist,
that they believe in the master race and rejoice in it. To be an
American, indeed, is automatically to be a racist—few find the
resources to escape.

Most blacks know this; few whites do. And it is *their* peculiar
fantasy to expect that centuries of racism can be undone pain-
lessly, that America can exist half free and half colonial, and that
this society can accept its blacks without a personal, institutional,
and social revolution. At this point a Riot Commission report, a
new civil-rights bill, a Labor Department grant to CORE, an
SCLC march on Washington, merely haul coals to Newcastle.
They are useless in heading off the gathering storm—pointless,
too late.

Whites simply have little grasp of the notion that their society
must change to be saved, that it must come to just terms with
those people everywhere whom it does not benefit—in other words,
its victims. And because whites do not understand this, two contingencies beckon like the crooked fingers of death: riot at home
and war abroad. Both are culminations of violence; both are logical outcomes of privilege won and maintained by jungle law.

The poor live under the threat of war, and since they know that
peace will never come from submission to war, they prepare to fight.

The rhetoric of the ghetto and the developing world is the rhetoric of war, whereas the rhetoric of the establishment is that of peace —while it wages war. The poor do not want war; it is forced upon them—a war not of their choice either in weapons or in tactics. Hunger, filth, early or living death—these are the weapons and tactics, backed up by the cruel weight of military force should they resist. But resist they will, and liberals, bemoaning violence and the prospect of more, will condemn it as reactionary and counterproductive—a luxury the poor cannot afford.

Meantime, the roots of war go unexplored, and the war-makers (including liberals) go untouched. Their power is as temporarily complete as it is ultimately self-defeating. They can refuse to seat the Mississippi Freedom Party, or they can produce the Tonkin Bay Resolution to attack North Vietnam—but only at the cost of angry and growing opposition from Americans and from former friends abroad. Consequently, the most unimaginable horrors become distinct possibilities: the destruction of America (and the world) through World War III or the destruction of America by its own people. Indeed, realism might require that one prefer the latter without necessarily eliminating the former, in the hope that internal chaos will make impossible America's economic and military presumptions abroad.

This is rather a brutal way of dealing with the signs of the times. One would like to handle them differently, except that the signs and the times are so exceptionally brutal. They are not brutal by accident, one must insist; they are brutal because our lives are so, and our lives are so because of a particularly ambiguous and deep-rooted philosophy that is at once distinctly Western and distinctly American. It is a syncretism developing from the impact of free-enterprise capitalism upon fundamentalist Christianity—a kind of moral positivism or empiricism.

More precisely, it is situation ethics controlled by perverted self-interest—personal selfishness at work publicly. It infects personal life, permeates institutions, dictates domestic and foreign policy, forms national purpose. Its expression is not just racism but other personal phenomena as bald or subtle: draftees fighting wars they do not understand, war critics filing tax returns to pay for overkill and Vietnam, professors teaching humanism and standing publicly for nothing, clerics vacillating between loyalty to country and that country's crimes.

Nationally, its expression in supercorporation and gross national product, self-censored press and credibility gap, Selective Service System and war profiteering. Internationally, it is "defensive" pact (NATO, CENTO, SEATO, and ANZUS), Vietnam, Green Berets in Guatemala, weapons systems that decrease national security (ABM)—in short, the problems *and* tragedies of empire.

To those who *know* black slavery and colonialization in this nation, Roy Wilkins and Whitney Young (or Thurgood Marshall and Ralph Bunche) are contemporary Booker T. Washingtons who have compromised the reality of being black to favor the establishment view of being black. That is, they neglect the morality of the question to stress its politics. They act more out of having "made it" than from a reaction to the miseries of blacks and the prejudices of whites. They are "integrated," to be sure; they are accepted as long as they remember where power lies and how much it will concede, and as long as they assent to the built-in racism of white power and move according to its terms.

Daniel Moynihan, however, is a case somewhat apart. As a white integrationist with impressive credentials, he performs a delicate liaison between white and black establishments, telling both just enough truth to keep them collaborating on programs designed to muffle black rage. His 1965 "Moynihan Report" is a case in point. It satisfied whites by implying racial inferiority and at the same time encouraged black hope that massive social services would help to stiffen their sagging family structure. But the end result was what William Ryan of Harvard called "Savage Discovery": Moynihan had discovered that blacks were savages who needed to be introduced gradually into the niceties of white civilization. The point was made, of course, at the expense of the real problem—the racial pathology of whites.

When one settles for the establishment, one settles for establishment values. It appears that the illusion of power held by card-carrying bureaucrats wheedles them into moral ambiguity, as though bureaucratic dynamics *were* the new morality. Lyndon

THE COLOR OF POVERTY

Johnson or Dean Rusk are clearly seen as extremes of this enigma; Hans Morgenthau, Walter Lippmann, and George Kennan as moderates. The latter three merely apply moderation to their moral relativism—they use more common sense, so to speak.

Morgenthau, for example, condemns the American intervention in Vietnam because of great-power "spheres of influence" that China should understandably share as a great power. America cannot profitably interfere with these spheres, he says, since interference will engender dangerous reaction, leaving us with the possible burden of policing the world. He believes that policy ought to be based, rather, on national interest. Such policy, however, leaves undisturbed the assumption that we can interfere where national interest *is* the fact—for example, in the Caribbean.

Lippmann opposed America's invasion of Santo Domingo because he felt that the danger of a Communist take-over had not been adequately proved. But what if it had? What if at another time and in similar circumstances intelligence was more accurate? What if the Communists were indigenous, and if they were not, what if the people still needed revolution? Opposition like Lippmann's opens the door for subsequent intervention where America has interests and where the threat of Communism is a fact.

Kennan, in turn, possesses a reputation for diplomatic experience and integrity, but his geopolitics concede to national interest consistently. Twice before the Senate Foreign Relations Committee he recommended de-escalation in Vietnam instead of throwing his considerable support behind the only viable and moral course—unilateral withdrawal. In light of our tendency even then to blunder ever deeper into the Vietnam morass, Kennan was no doubt persuaded that his responsibility lay with a recommendation for "the possible." But what moderate nationalists deem "possible" has a curious way of being substantially immoral, with ultimately tragic consequences. One outraged listener remarked after hearing Kennan give his Norton Lectures at Harvard in 1961, "He didn't seem to know the difference between right and wrong."

It is difficult to say whether he does or not; it is easier to say that American political morality is one that power makes right. It is the morality of a sophisticated jungle, whether national or international, simply because it allows its advocates to be moral chameleons who can switch from principle to pragmatism with the footwork of a dancing-master. American national interest provides the yardstick, and its measurement is flexible enough to include without contradiction "bombing North Vietnam back to the Stone Age" (General Curtis LeMay and Representative L. Mendel Rivers) and a halt in the bombings, de-escalation, and negotiation (Senators Fulbright and Robert Kennedy). In other words, American *realpolitik* permits a range of option concerning greater or lesser degrees of exported barbarity. What degree best serves national interest? This is the overriding issue.

Real issues are not allowed to intrude in any relevant way, and neither establishment "left" nor "right" will dare talk of them seriously. Such issues would be the dominance exercised over national life by economics, technology as benefit and as threat, militarism in a civilian society, public morality in national and foreign affairs, the rights of life and of national sovereignty enjoyed by other peoples. Another would be the reality of revolution in an affluent society.

Questions like these are today of a life-and-death variety, yet bureaucrats shy away from them, like Rotarians from revolutionaries. And since they do, public debate remains hopelessly confused and infantile, and little public support emerges for humane and reasonable policies—unilateral withdrawal from Vietnam, restitution to the Vietnamese, acceptance of Communist China into the United Nations, cessation of the international sale of arms, disarmament initiatives to assist nuclear nonproliferation. When an ethos of power becomes public policy, national interests cannot serve human interests. And the ultimate question, whether life can continue in a human way on this planet, is not honestly faced.

At any rate, the fact exists that moral empiricism gives philosophical support to the historical racism of the West and to the racist flavor implicit in America's imperial ambitions. Moral empiricism is the philosophy of the Western nation-state, tenaciously and ruthlessly enough held to have ideological fervor and thrust. That it has sponsored from the Christian West the various nuances of imperialist greed—racism, neo-colonialism, economic rapacity, war, untold millions ruined and dead—seems of little account to most. Ironically, it still bears the label of political realism.

By and large, moral empiricism is a status philosophy cultivated by attachment to privilege. And the policy that springs from it treats the world's poor as objects of manipulation and aggrandizement. With Japan as the only notable colored exception in the world, whites are powerful, colored powerless; whites are the imperialists (or neo-colonialists), colored the subjects; whites are "haves," colored "have-nots"; whites few, colored many. Going beyond the racial overtones in the actual war with Vietnam and the virtual war with China, it is true to state that a wider war has already begun, cutting across national and ideological lines—a war between embattled North Atlantic whites (and Russians) and the oppressed-world colored.

The correspondence between color and poverty has produced a phrase—"the color of poverty." Seven out of ten men live in abject poverty, most of them colored people. Inevitably, color and want set up a fellowship that makes fidelities like culture and nationalism or attractions like Communism or democracy somewhat marginal. In other words, Commonwealth blacks in Malawi, with a $30 per capita yearly income, have much more in common with impoverished South American peons and Vietnamese peasants than with white Canadians with a yearly income of $1,600. Britons love to refer to the Commonwealth "family," but it is one of fancy more than of fact, or it is a family of poor and rich relations.

In effect, the four hungers of the developing world—hunger of the stomach, hunger for freedom, hunger for employment, and hunger for culture—are shared by Indians, Chinese, Guatemalans, Congolese, Ghanians, Haitians, Bolivians, and hundreds of millions like them. Color and poverty meet in these people and bind them together. Their common cause stems from a common urgency of condition—a cause of emancipation and freedom which is energized by the dynamics of despair, awareness, and pride.

Emancipation and freedom mean eventual conflict on a mas-

sive, world scale; the developing world is too great a profit item
to be relinquished freely and justly by the West. Self-determination has always been an expensive process, both to those who demand it by right and to those who must allow it by duty. In every
corner of the globe racial lines are becoming distinct and turbulent. Initially, the ostracism of colored came from the whites;
now its reaction is seen—the rejection of whites by colored. The
result is race war, now noticeable in its horrid preliminaries in
American cities, in South Africa and Rhodesia, in Angola and Mozambique, in Vietnam and Hong Kong, in Guatemala and Peru.[8]

The world now recognizes Africa as the cradle of human development, as a continent that was extraordinarily advanced in
the quality of government, art, and trade while Europe was fighting its way back from the Roman collapse. Ties of culture and
trade kept Africa close to the East, but economic profit created
an interest in Africa for European whites. Cheap labor meant
slaves, so race war had its first ominous roots in Africa.

Whites robbed Africa of its people, transported them through
half the world, and set themselves up as masters of the black man
in the black man's home. Whites exploited Africans successively
as slave traders, colonialists, governors, overseers, and finally as
extenders of loans after independence or as stubborn defenders
of white supremacy. In terms of equality, African blacks have
now won a paper status (excepting South Africa, Rhodesia, Angola, and Mozambique); but in terms of equality's technological
power and the means to power, both of which are largely white
preserves, very little has changed.

Whites in Central and South America—mostly Spanish and Portuguese, some English and French—liberally sowed the area with
African slaves. With far less scrupulosity than their neighbors to
the north, *and* far less hypocrisy, whites cohabited enthusiastically
with blacks and Indians to make of the continent a veritable
hodgepodge of human color. Later, when control was slowly
wrested from the declining Europeans—not by peons but by the
frustrated "free" class—South American countries embarked upon
an endless series of bloody revolutions during which one *caudillo*

replaced another, leaving the poor virtually unchanged in their misery.

It was at this point that the United States entered as a substitute for European power. Using the Monroe Doctrine as legal cover, and frankly confident in a badly disguised imperial role, Northern economic encroachments spread rapidly (often backed by Marines), so that today South America is a giant economic fief of the United States. White rape of the area, which began with plundered treasure and the plantation holdings of the Europeans, now operates under Northern auspices, but with little of the candid rapacity of the Europeans.

Consistently enough, color blindness is strenuously proclaimed. But it is a myth. Black men, mulattoes, Indians, and dark-skinned *mestizos* are the South American poor, whether as low-paid serfs on the vast plantations or as unemployed outcasts in the wretched city slums. As elsewhere in a white-dominated world, color is related to economic power—ruling class, white; middle class, light-skinned; proletariat, colored. And the white ruling class consists of native satraps of the United States.

In perfectly logical fashion, discrimination against blacks in the United States was matched by discrimination against other colored—Indians, Chinese, and Japanese. Harried and slaughtered by settlers and troops, herded onto reservations or driven inexorably west, robbed even of their reservation land in some cases, Indians have declined from a precolonial estimate of 850,000 to less than half that number. Extermination may not have been the conscious intent, but it has come close to becoming fact. Even more than blacks, American Indians are casualties of native racism—dispiriting reminders of our unfinished racial business.

Chinese in the West fared better racially than Indians, principally because their patriarchal culture strongly resisted assimilation, and because this country had a responsibility to China for their welfare. With the completion of the railroads, however, the Pacific became a one-way street between China and the United States. Despite the profits coming from an open-door policy in China, Washington checked immigration and denied naturalization to the Chinese already here. Our original Chinese Exclusion Act, which shut down emigration to these shores, our hopes for a democratic China during and after World War II, our fierce resentment against the Chinese Revolution, our successful efforts to keep Communist China out of the United Nations—all suggest a policy of greed, arrogance, and stupidity largely racist in origin.

The Japanese, who first came to the United States about 1880, encountered prejudice well tested against the Chinese. After the century's turn and with the emergence of Japan as a great power, racist paranoia deepened, and Americans began to beat the drum of "Yellow Peril." Harassed by several Alien Land Acts, denied citizenship by naturalization, and confined to ghettos, the Japanese had numerically declined when the disaster of Pearl Harbor struck. Despite consistent efforts to study America and to follow its patterns, despite the native citizenship of two-thirds of all American Japanese, despite an absence of any sabotage in either America or Hawaii, despite unquestionable loyalty, 110,000 men, women, and children were thrown into internment camps for the duration of World War II.

Whites of the British Commonwealth learned their racism through imperialism, however tattered the panoply of their empire today. Racism is for them, as for others, one of the luxuries of power—a package combining the contempt for the colored which arises from colonization, and the Anglo-Saxon distrust of foreigners, especially black foreigners. Evidence of racial discrimination abounds in the Commonwealth world—in Australia and New Zealand, where the fear of the yellow and brown masses to the north prompts anticolored immigration legislation and support for America's Vietnam war; in South Africa and Rhodesia (former Commonwealth members), which so far have been successful in resisting independence for the oppressed and bitter black majorities; in England itself, where West Indian immigration since World War II has provoked widespread and sometimes violent resentment.

Another factor feeding Commonwealth racism is Britain's powerlessness to support its federation with military protection—a fact that puts pressure on the Commonwealth countries to accept

American imperialism and to avail themselves of its military cover. Commonwealth solidarity is therefore more of an identification with the United States than with England, whose military weakness directs it toward the same course.

Whites of the Soviet Union, in contrast to other whites, had little opportunity to learn racial discrimination from colonialism. What contributed to their racism was a fixation with a world Communist movement directed to the overthrow of class systems. To a very large extent racism was written into the movement, and the virtual failure of that movement entrenched the racism. In the United States, for example, Marxists alienated black leaders by loyalty to the Comintern rather than to black rights. With undeviating obedience to Moscow's "line," Communists called upon blacks to support Stalin's sale of oil to Mussolini, who was then attacking Ethiopia; to support both Russia and Germany following the Hitler-Stalin pact; and to support only Russia when Germany attacked it later in World War II. For these reasons, mainly, Marcus Garvey rejected Communism very early, to be followed later by the NAACP and A. Philip Randolph.

With impressive consistency, Russian Communists confirmed their mistakes abroad by discriminating against African and Asian students studying in the Soviet Union. This discrimination was not entirely due to prejudice; a coercive social system was also at fault. But the fact is that these students were not allowed a reasonable integration into Russian life. They could not see and judge what they pleased; they could not choose or reject custom, as the Russians did, or associate with Russian women.

It is far easier for people and countries to rationalize failure toward blacks than to face the failure *and* its consequences. Frequently, therefore, whites will offer evidence of racial "progress" in the United States and abroad: most of Africa independent and the rest on its way, strengthened civil-rights legislation in America, Algeria's victory over France, China's rise as a great colored nation. Evidence like this ignores, however, the fact that two world wars and a communications revolution did far more to raise expectations in the colored world than did white altruism. If whites allowed independence, they frowned upon revolution;

capitalism puts a far higher value on social stability than on the elimination of massive social abuse. If racial gains have been won since World War II, it is because colored people have insisted upon them and only at a tremendous price of struggle and blood.

By a sort of affluent opacity, white nations fail to see that their refusal of responsibility toward the colored world and their fierce opposition to social revolution there increase the certainty of racial war. There seems little comprehension of the injustice done and of the terrible harvest of violence which the injustice is now beginning to reap. Whites have separated sowing from harvesting, and if they will admit that the seeds are a debasing poverty and vast economic gaps, they will not admit that the harvest must be revolution and war. Too long has the harvest meant profits alone, and for the white world only.

In this atmosphere of suspicion, unrest, and repression, world trends suggest that the West—especially the United States—will unite with the Soviet Union to police the world. Such an alliance might be years away, however, due to the profound American distrust of Communism, and the present conviction that this nation can, without help, pacify the areas within its economic interest. In turn, the Soviet Union cannot abandon without cost an ideology dedicated theoretically to a classless world society—an ideology compromised more and more by Russia's rising prosperity. Obviously, any abrupt move to ally with the West would irrevocably destroy Russia's waning leadership of the Communist bloc, deepen its rift with Communist China, and widen gaps with the poor (colored) world. Nonetheless, a harmony of view has developed between the United States and Russia concerning the threat of China, and this view may eventually prove reason enough for a united front.

China—enigmatic, careful, and astute in its leadership, and apprehensively regarded by the white world—is now emerging as the hope of the developing world, and for several reasons: She is colored, she is poor, and she has sold herself impressively as favoring revolution and those who need it, rather than identifying herself exclusively with her own national interest (the Russian mistake). Indeed, China offers to the colored world the only full-scale example of social revolution with which it can identify—an example backed by considerable respect for self-determination and by liberal amounts (for a poor country) of money and technical help. This is not to say that Asians, Africans, and South Americans accept Maoism uncritically, or that they disregard the terrible paroxysms it has caused. It is to say that the world's colored poor see in China what revolution can accomplish to erase the humiliations suffered under white dominance and to provide the leverage for equality and hope. And if China's ideology, suspension of liberties, and sporadic violence are regarded with aversion, China's sympathy for the "color" of want is not.

It would be irresponsible to ignore the central position of the United States in this momentous black-white struggle on every frontier of the world. If ever a society was endowed with the potentials of hope for itself and for mankind, it is ours. Yet we have failed miserably to use them; far from offering hope to others, we do not have it ourselves. We who have the most wealth have also the least hope.

Perhaps we suspect Lenin was right, or perhaps we cannot resist proving him right, when he said that war comes from pressures inherent in the capitalist system and from its fight for markets. Whatever the case, our conservatism matches our wealth, simply because stability guarantees what we now possess and favors the accumulation of more. In addition, stability must be as general as investment, which is to say that both must be worldwide. Or so we tend to see it.

In this context anti-Communism is little more than an ideology to support the American infatuation with holdings, and with the security and power which holdings supposedly insure. Attachment to ideology—or to militarism—is like attachment to wealth. Each is turned on more easily than it is turned off. In all likelihood, therefore, America will continue to label world revolution as Communist subversion, will continue to identify with fascist regimes, will continue to equivocate confusedly with legitimate aspirations, until both the urban scene and the world scene erupt in a crescendo of riot and war.

And as sauce to the meat, there are our vaunted ABC (atomic, bacteriological, and chemical) weapons, in which we have put our trust as the ultimate stabilizing factor, but which are in fact obscene blackmail, the symbol of moral rot, and the paradox of fading security, and militance is in effect an admission that we have no power but wealth and the arms to defend it. Hence justice or injustice in using power is no longer an issue. We have consequently arrived at that absurd point of inflexibility where control has shifted from us to our technology, from us to our possessions.

It is not enough to say that power is both benefit and responsibility; it is more important to ask why our power is irresponsible. Until we face this question, we have no answers save our weapons—faint security indeed when mutual enemies can burn down a world in a matter of hours and days. As long as we seduce ourselves into believing that security can spring from injustice, or that British subservience or Russian moderation or rosters of mercenaries are any proof at all of justice, so long will the conviction remain that we are right, and so long will we throw fuel on the bonfire.

What our blacks want, just as the colored of the developing world want, is a human relationship that proves itself by justice. They do not want our pity, our charity, our dole, our neuroses, or our almost habitual viciousness toward people. They want us not as we are nor as we give, but as we ought to be and as we ought to give.

The time has passed when the black ghettos of America or the colored countries of the world can be bought off by the Office of Economic Opportunity or the Agency for International Development, with their funds carefully allotted to smother unrest. Newark, Detroit, Vietnam, Guatemala, Peru, Rhodesia, and the Arab world are now on the sharp edge of revolution, as stubborn and relentless in its momentum as the white power seeking to suppress it.

What this movement tells us as it ominously gains anger and force is that being human is a claim upon all peoples and all property, and that no race, nation, or regional coalition has an arbitrary right to gather, restrict, or abuse the means to being human. What this movement tells us is that all men and what they own are common riches, common resources, and subject to a common use. Finally, what this movement tells us, not as threat but as desperate omen, is that the colored will no longer stand for inhumanity in whites, any more than they will stand for deprivation in themselves. And the cry that comes from their misery and anger is also a kind of plea: "Let us admit our common poverty, and in doing that, we can make one another rich men."

Manifestos of revolution proliferate in an age like ours, some of them helpful, some of them not. One of the more popular is Frantz Fanon's *Wretched of the Earth*. Fanon was a black psychoanalyst from Martinique who joined the Algerians in their struggle against the French. From this experience came a synthesis of revolution at once obscure and magnificent. He refers to the Pauline concept of the "new man" to express both his fierce dedication to that promise, and his rejection of a Christianity that has failed it.

We must leave our dreams and abandon our old beliefs and friendships of the time before life began. Let us waste no time in sterile litanies and nauseating mimicry. Leave this Europe where they are never done talking about Man, yet murder men everywhere they find them, at the corner of every one of their streets, in all the corners of the globe. For centuries they have stifled almost the whole of humanity in the name of so-called spiritual experience. Look at them today swaying between atomic and spiritual disintegration. . . .

Europe undertook the leadership of the world with ardour, cynicism and violence. . . . Europe has declined all humility and all modesty; but she has also set her face against all solicitude and all tenderness.

She has only shown herself parsimonious and niggardly where men are concerned; it is only men that she has killed and devoured. . . .

Two centuries ago, a former European colony decided to catch up with Europe. It succeeded so well that the United States of America became a monster, in which the taints, the sickness and the inhumanity of Europe have grown to appalling dimensions. . . .

No, we do not want to catch up with anyone. What we want to do is to go forward all the time, night and day, in the company of Man, in the company of all men. The caravan should not be stretched out, for in that case each line will hardly see those who precede it; and men who no longer recognize each other meet less and less together, and talk to each other less and less.

It is a question of the Third World starting a new history of Man, a history which will have regard to the sometimes prodigious theses which Europe has put forward but which will also not forget Europe's crimes, of which the most horrible was committed in the heart of man, and consisted of the pathological tearing apart of his functions and the crumbling away of his unity. . . .

For Europe, for ourselves and for humanity, comrades, we must turn over a new leaf, we must work out new concepts, and try to set afoot a new man.[9]

III

The Fire
This Time?

a cat said
on the corner

the other day
dig man

how come so many
of us
niggers

are dying over there
in that white
man's war

they say more of us
are dying

than them peckerwoods
& it just don't make sense

unless it's true
that the honkeys

are trying to kill us out
with the same stone

they killing them other cats
with

you know, he said
two birds with one stone
     —CLARENCE MAJOR, "Vietnam #1"

TWO STORIES BRING PAST AND PRESENT TO-
gether in the pain and convulsion of America's black revolution.
Lerone Bennett, a black historian, tells the first, and it is a para-
ble:

The Patriot, attended by a "faithful" Negro slave, climbed a steep
mountain and tempted fate with a cry of FREEDOM! The word bounced
off the craggy rocks and came back in a resounding echo: FREEDOM!
FREEDOM! The echo was so close, so menacing, that the Patriot turned
quickly to see if the slave had spoken. But the slave was silent or
seemed to be silent. The Patriot lifted his head and shouted again:
FREEDOM! FREEDOM! And an echo came back: FREEDOM! FREEDOM! The
Patriot drew back in fear. Was he imagining things? Or did the slave
speak? In desperation, the Patriot railed at the rocks and commanded
the words to stop. But the words echoed and reechoed in the mountain
air. The words swelled and swallowed the original sound, assuming a
texture and a life of their own, reverberating from peak to peak in a
continuous curtain of sound. In mounting fear, the Patriot shut his ears
against the words of his own mouth. He stood thus, ears stopped and
eyes closed, unable to climb to the peak or go down to the valley, a
tragic figure paralyzed by the cry he had raised and the reality he had
made. Shadows gathered in the crevices, and, at length, darkness fell
on the high and dangerous ledge where two men—one white and one
colored, one slave and one free—stood face to face, uneasily watching
and measuring each other, listening with bated breath to the sounds of
freedom reverberating in the thin dry air.[1]

The second comes from the summer of 1967—the words of a
young Boston rioter who had no job, no high-school education,
no card in a civil-rights organization, and who crossed no state
line to riot:

It's not the "agitators" who blow up. It's us, all over the place, the colored people who say it's too late for us to wait and wait when nothing comes anyway. Every black man knows he's not really wanted, just put up with, and given the salad while Whitey gets the turkey. So we're all one, by being black; that's why we get hot in the summer and try to break out, and break in, or something, even if we're in Iowa—like the papers say, it's all over the same. I'm just living here, and when I heard the police was doing what they was, I said to myself, they're sticking another knife into us, and if we try to defend ourselves they call us animals, so I'd better go fight . . . I mean fight beside my brothers . . . so I just went there, and the action was going on, and that's how I got into it. There was lots of us there—must have been a thousand, they said. And inside our people said, "Good!" They didn't want the damage and the hurt, but they wanted to tell Whitey off, even if they couldn't do it themselves. Answers? I don't know. That's your job. You know what's needed and you probably say it can't be done now, because there are other things that are wanting your money. Well, you go believe that; but don't expect us to, and don't be surprised when we don't.[2]

Two men still measure one another, one white, one black, and the issue between them is still freedom, or their *mutual* slavery. White looks at black and says, "You're black, and we don't want you!" or "You're not ready!" or "We're doing all we can, and there's no money!" or "What do you people want?" or "Cool it, or we'll clean you out!" Black looks at white and says, "Integration with you isn't worth it, but we'll get justice through you or over you!" or "We're ready, but you aren't!" or "There's money if you'd stop killing colored people overseas!" or "We won't cool it; this is just the beginning!" or "We want what you're afraid of—freedom!"

Such is the nature of our racial impasse. One can justly call it "impasse" because both sides have nearly irreconcilable views of the changes needed to reconcile differences and reduce tensions. While ordinary white pathologies have been further complicated by the corrupting influence of the Vietnam war and by the summer riots, black expectations continue to leap and solidify with those of colored revolutionaries around the globe. Pressures upon whites to defend themselves or to suppress blacks grow apace, while pressures upon blacks to force entry into society—or failing that, to burn it down—mount accordingly. Civilization or a social jungle seems the choice. George Bernard Shaw's tart comment that America was the only nation he knew which had gone from barbarism to decadence without trying civilization seems very much the point.

Both races call for change from a purity dictated by their positions. In effect, whites tell blacks to change—to forget realizations of contempt, misery, and injustice; to purge resentment and anger; to keep black colonies somnolent and grateful, waiting patiently for a better time that never comes. Meanwhile, blacks tell whites to change—to remember, as they remember, humiliation, brutality, lynching, rape, and fire; to remember all the broken promises, all the pious cant, all the hypocrisy and treachery. Blacks say, "Learn to remember as we do, and you will change."

But one has to experience to remember; or failing experience, one must live a life sharing common elements with men everywhere, no matter what their race or class. In other words, one must have some basis for change, some resources that clearly reveal a need for change and impart a desire to have it. It is in these resources that our society is fast becoming bankrupt, and one is not necessarily making America a whipping boy to claim it. Racism is one of the many prices we pay for affluence, and as a species of violence, racism is being profoundly reinforced as mentality and way of life by other species of violence under American sponsorship around the world. Technically, we may be able to carry out a foreign police-action while grappling with domestic problems like racism, but technical abilities are unfortunately dependent upon the will of the people to use them. This will we do not have, as the defeat of civil-rights legislation in 1966 proves; as Congressional derision toward a modest antirat bill proves; as the enormous unpopularity of the O.E.O. proves. In this one question at least, Congress is an accurate sounding-board for the nation.

It is nonetheless impossible to deal with the overall complexities of our current social and international dilemmas. One must rather isolate them one by one and then attempt to see each of them as different species of American violence (injustice)—violence that makes America not the world's hope (as Americans have long considered it to be), but the primary threat to the world's peace. We are, it would appear, at the point now where we must fish or cut bait in both Vietnam and in our cities. And if cutting bait means a heartrending evaluation of national purpose, institutional life, and moral commitment, it is certainly preferable to continued fishing, which is slowly drawing our people into the horror of domestic rebellion, and the world's people into the abyss of war. Pope Paul has remarked that the world is sick, and Senator Fulbright has said that our society is sick. Without begging the question, it may be possible to show that racism helps to make it so, since racism is a sickness with which most white Americans have been inoculated and in which they have been schooled.

It should not be necessary to prove that racism is a personal and social pathology. It is necessary, however, to convince most white Americans that they are heirs to it, and victims of it. Furthermore, it is fully as necessary to convince whites that racism is a psychology (or pathology) of violence which destroys them under its own slavery in the same proportion as it destroys blacks. In effect, racism checks or ruins the freedom of its perpetrators while doing exactly the same thing (in a different way) to its victims. Finally, it is necessary to show how racism is a disease that is fast becoming an affluent luxury (or curse), in that whites see it as both a contribution to their affluence and a reason for keeping them affluent. In this sense, racism persists as the psychological counterpart of a bank vault.

It takes no great imagination to see an identification between the tortured thinking of a racist and black-ghetto turmoil, or what Bayard Rustin calls the "riotous rebellions" in our cities. The latter is merely the concrete expression of its spiritual cause. Until this nation seriously encounters racial prejudice with all the force of its governmental, institutional, and social vigor; until its doctors begin to regard racism with the same concern with which they view other neurotic and psychotic illnesses; until its churches and synagogues begin to demand both atonement for racial crimes and evidence of interracial compassion as qualifications for membership; until both labor and management pursue massive programs of compensatory membership and hiring; until our country at large sees the racist as a public enemy; until America, in short, dedicates itself to the pain and insecurity of converting national consciousness and conscience, then measures favoring blacks are bound to be halfhearted and inadequate, and the violence of riot is apt to be followed by the violence of revolution.

It must be seen, therefore, that the fundamental focus in race relations should not be concern over swollen inner-city areas; not social science and its preoccupation with data about black people; not viable poverty programs and their funding and staffing; not concern about the Church and its service to black people; not firm and consistent leadership by the President and Congress. Rather, the focus should be the racism in the minds and hearts of white people, for only the removal of this racism will make truly effective measures possible.

In other words, America ought to be concerned with why its white people largely think that blackness makes people different and less, that straight hair is better than nappy hair, that an aquiline nose is better than a broad one, that whites ought to live with whites and marry whites, that blacks are sexually precocious but mentally retarded, and that only whites are capable of industry, thrift, and creative contribution. Astoundingly enough, such childish myths and vicious prejudgments are at the root of a crisis that can tear this country apart. It has already begun to do so. Black people surely do not like us playing God any better than God does.

To confront our emotional and psychic disorders in race relations is to confront ourselves and to ask the critical question, "What manner of man am I?" And to confront ourselves is to win a small measure of freedom, with a promise of more. It is to be slowly capable of asking with clear gaze and mounting strength questions like these: Why are our inner cities black colonies of filth and despair, and why are they likely to remain so without massive applications, not of money, but of humanity? Why are human resources considered even less important in antipoverty measures than adequate funding? Why has established religion taken only the most faltering and indecisive moves relative to poverty and black people? Why has the Government, after moving into a vacuum of leadership in human rights, been forced to retreat? Why are the black-rights groups now split in philosophy and action, each with its own kind of desperation? Why does white America have a perfect genius for adjusting to every black hope and initiative in such a way that the black masses remain steeped in misery and bitterness?

If whites continue to disregard with blatant contempt the moral aspects of race relations (as most whites do) and to concentrate fearfully on buying off or dampening down black-ghetto anger (as most whites do), it is safe to say that the black lumpen proletariat will reject submission, tolerance, and nonviolence in the face of myriad instances of white violence against blacks. And blacks will do this more and more en masse, with better organization of arson and firepower, even at the price of seeing their homes destroyed and their people killed.

Most assuredly, the question of whether America must endure a running guerrilla war in its cities, internecine in viciousness and scope, is not in black hands at all. The question depends upon the white choice of withdrawing from the violent provocation and oppression of blacks, which at this point in history is simply intolerable. But somber reflections come to mind: Power once gained is not relinquished; profit from the poor is not abandoned; history gives few (if any) examples of conversion within great nations. Let the reader himself weigh the present, and from his hope, help to form the future.

Be that as it may, any human and Christian sense requires the exposure of the sheer deceit and unwarranted assumptions infesting most white discussions of black rights in America. Irresponsibility toward Negroes is seldom admitted because a banal self-righteousness constitutes the white defense; there is no consciousness of guilt or of the need for restitution. How often one is left with the sinking feeling after discussing race relations with middle-class whites that here are people who must have their nigger or go mad. The question then becomes, What is to be done with the violence normally reserved for blacks? Available scapegoats very often keep others "normal" and "contributing" members of society.

Another refuge from reality and from responsible association
with blacks is the white conception of power as the weapon of
rule and class. When "Black Power" was first heard on James
Meredith's Mississippi march, it was articulated (as it largely is
now) according to a reverse definition of white power, which
gains preference for special-interest blocs through a variety of
economic and political tools. Included in this, of course, was a
factor loosely held to by black militants: a black imitation of the
traditional racial exclusivism practiced by whites. Black Power
was the only sensible response to a racist white society that had
substantially agreed to put off indefinitely the question of black
rights. The *quid pro quo,* in terms of the system, would seem to
be eminently fair; at the very least, it possessed an utter consistency with what had been done by whites.

But a nerve center had been pressed, and white outcries were
anguished, loud, and frantic. Black Power generated a sense of
furious outrages, couched in the moralistic rhetoric of guilty, be-
wildered, and threatened people. An incredible bloc of reaction-
aries, fence-sitters, and liberals emerged, including a number of
black leaders who were increasingly caught between civil-rights
failure and white monolithic power. White reflexes went like this
(though publicized versions were not nearly so crude): "They"
(not us) want to be separate; "they" (not us) want economic
power and political voice; "they" (not us) want to control "their"
lives and fortunes. But why? There was no ability to answer, only
the rankling suspicion that the colonials were breaking out, and
doing it in a typically vicious, native way. Guilt told whites that
revenge was the motive; sexual hang-up said "they" want our
women; economic status said "they" want our jobs.

The furor over Black Power helps to explode another white
pretension—lawfulness toward blacks. White power is maintained
not only by wealth and majority membership but by the law as
well, and the law is often interpreted to favor power and is often
violated to defend power. If one wishes to examine white power's
debt to law, one need but recall the Civil Rights Era and the
hundreds of legal cases it produced. By and large, these involved

the clear rights of black plaintiffs or protesting civil-rights workers, yet many cases received adverse rulings, and many had to be
appealed at enormous expense and disadvantage, thus conveying
an unavoidable implication of the law as the tool of the *status
quo*. In a still more flagrant manner, whites violate with impunity
open-housing and fair-employment legislation; white slumlords
violate building codes; white Mafia figures organize crime in the
ghetto: drugs, numbers, prostitution, and an astounding variety
of rackets. In view of the unremitting and massive lawlessness of
whites toward blacks—quiet, unpublicized, done more by rule than
exception—even the black crime rate or the legal violations resulting from urban riots are paltry by comparison. Indeed, white
lawlessness is largely the cause of black lawlessness.

What is the basis, one might ask, for racial pathology so stubbornly tenacious, so virulent and destructive? What has so infected our consciousness that we can ignore in blacks the common
attributes of humanity and be obsessed with their surface differences from whites? An inheritance of racial mythology, which defined historically means the class system separating whites from
blacks, is one answer. A "thing"-dominated society is another;
white-centered education and bland, superstitious religion are
others. These and similar evils combine to form in us the convictions that black men must be dirty because they are black, must be
immoral because they are criminal, must be retarded because they
are uneducated, must be promiscuous because they bear their
children and rear them. And when in reality blacks are obviously
clean, moral, educated, and chaste, phobias against blackness still
prevail, and acceptance is grudging, halfhearted, and suspicious.

So we capsulize our delusions and fears and moral imbecility
into what is called the Negro problem, and by a sick set of mental
gymnastics we lay the whole suppurating burden on black backs
and call it theirs. In effect, however, there is no black "problem";
black people have only human problems of adaptation to a white
master-race complex that stunts its owners in a kind of moral and
emotional preschool where an Aryanism of caste is taught. Here
the "problem" rests, and while it rests there undisturbed and un-

suspected, whites are helpless to do other than to destroy blacks, and themselves. To speak from such a classroom, therefore, and to say to blacks, "What can we do for you?" is to ignore both the school and the crippled graduate. Somehow, the schooling must change, and the price for that is high.

America is very far from paying the price. In fact, there is appallingly little perception that a price must be paid. Within its power structure, this nation pursues the elusive goal of racial harmony with no significant attempt to understand its own history or to analyze its national purpose or to weigh the quality of its domestic and international life. Since this is so, national response to black rage and riot remains irrevocably wedded to the logic of national rationale, scheme, and system, all of which tend to reinforce and defend themselves. In America rhetoric has long served as a harmless substitute for free speech. Consequently, when mountains of verbal and printed rhetoric on race flow from Washington, pulpit, and press, one is reminded more of white malaise than of white willingness to change. For who can deny that change means revolution—revolution of a most unique and priceless type—revolution that seizes the fading nonviolence of blacks and makes it credo and life?

One can of course continue to hope for the eventuality of an authentic change in whites without really believing in its probability. It is in fact more than likely that America will confirm its historic decision to outlaw blacks, and to outlaw them indefinitely. Most blacks now live in what has been called occupied territory, where they are natives under colonial rule, where white presence is preponderantly exploitative or repressive. It is no secret that black ghettos finance disproportionate segments of white affluence, and that white luxury is very often paid for by black misery.

Within black stockades exploitation becomes possible through repression, and repression is police business. This point was made clear by a remarkable white sergeant of the New York City police who still serves in a Harlem precinct. "Most of us," he said to me, "know why we're here. Almost none of us think it's wrong. Generally, we do two jobs. We protect the bloodsuckers, and we uh. . . . Bloodsuckers? Hell, anyone who grabs the black buck here—the syndicate guys who sell dope, numbers, and black women; loan sharks, rent collectors, insurance salesmen, con men, phonies of all kinds. They're parasites, see? We look out for them, and they help us do the second job that I was gonna tell you about. They help us keep Harlem quiet, you understand? They keep the people screwed up, and that keeps them quiet. Keeping them quiet means keeping them here. You get it? *Here!*" He repeated the word while jabbing at the sidewalk with a forefinger.

White parasites in a black ghetto may not necessarily see it that way, nor may the overlord parasites who send some of them there. Most of the overlords would disdain coming to a place like Harlem except to wonder at the strange anguish of Negro jazz or to follow their mysterious lust for black women. But the net effect is the same, and the cause is greed. Black ghettos are helpless, and they are therefore susceptible to rape. What was done by white colonists all over the colored world has become the rule in black colonies here: Test native strength, choke it if necessary, and make it pay its tribute.

In the most practical sense, therefore, blacks must live according to white whim and nod, and whim and nod spring fundamentally from the economics of a color-caste system. Year by year the frosting from the black cake is scraped off and fed to the white world—to the extent that a black elite is allowed emolument but not acceptance. (Which brings to mind the tolerance of British colonialism, wherein control rested with a native elite, at no expense to profits.) Meanwhile, the black masses fester in the rotten city-core, their lives an involuntary and hideous product of ruthless caste-economics. Depending on the locale, black unemployment is two, three, five, and eight times the white average; on a per capita basis, blacks earn half of what whites earn; black college-graduates earn two-thirds as much as white college-graduates. Against all expectations and the evidence of tangible progress, this is a condition that is worsening in the most inexorable fashion—because of impoverished education, because of lily-white trade unions, because of cybernation, because, above all,

the syndrome of poverty is so powerful that only a few excep-
tional individuals are able to overcome it. And this occurs in spite
of a swollen war-economy and an unparalleled gross national income.

Americans have an ingrained and profoundly reverent attitude
toward money and the power identified with money. It is very
nearly a national axiom that money can buy most of what is important and can control most of what is not. Therefore, keeping
blacks in their place, keeping them colonial clients and perpetual
scapegoats, keeping them from power and from forcing an accommodation to power, is purely and simply keeping them poor.

Inextricably tied to black poverty as partial cause and partial
effect is the deprived education accorded most blacks in this country. (Interestingly enough, some critics do not hesitate to call it
educational genocide.) If we recognize that educational institutionalism is an integral servant of national priorities, the classroom
training of blacks can be seen in its intent to keep them both in
and out of the system—in the system, because the educational rationale used for both blacks and whites is essentially the same;
out of it, because the quality of education offered both is vastly
different.

To put it another way, local education is roughly of the quality
that local power demands it should be. When local power is
powerless because it is poor, when in addition it combines its
poverty with blackness, what it commands as education is a very
poor disguise indeed. More accurately, education for most black
children is really one of the more powerful instruments of servitude, since it conveys as fact the myth of what America is not,
rather than what it is; since it ignores history, black contributions,
black rights; and since it prepares students for the black under-
belly of American society—all with a designed lethargy and in-
eptitude. The celebrated "separate but equal" facilities of the
South are in fact the national pattern, and there is no denying
their success in remaining separate but hardly equal. Harold
Howe, the U.S. Commissioner of Education, refers rather despairingly to thirteen years of "progress" in the integration of edu-

cation since the Supreme Court decision of 1954. On a national average, white high-school students have over nine out of ten classmates from their own group. One can give due credit to Federal attempts to enforce the law without avoiding nausea at its lack of success. If classroom integration is a fundamental sign of equal facility and opportunity, *de facto* segregation in the classroom is nonetheless as fully pronounced as in 1954.

One can possibly suppose at this point a similar pattern in housing, which will be, by the very nature of racism, the last rampart to fall. For a variety of reasons, however, there is more segregated housing in America than in 1954, nor have Executive orders, Federal financing, Northern fair-housing legislation, and the Civil Rights Bills of 1964 and 1965 done much to affect the stubborn pattern.

Home has a symbolic content for most Americans; it means much more to them than housing. Immersed as they are in free-enterprise capitalism, and knowing as they do that capitalism is enterprising but not free, Americans cling to private property as the only unequivocal fruit of the system, the only one that is precisely what it says it is: "private," "property," and "mine." As such, it is a refuge against the very disturbing evidence that in public or in a profession a man is being used by things, that he is a mere gear in the social machinery, that he really counts for very little. At home he can be a radically different person. There he can pretend to control his life; he can salve his violated pride and assert his manhood. There the world is made to stop, or it is allowed to enter only if it is stripped of its jarring elements and filtered in through TV fantasies and convivial neighbors, relatives, and friends. An accurate suspicion exists that the home is a therapeutic haven that can energize one's tired and assaulted psyche, preparing it to return to a hostile and bewildering world.

All things being equal, blacks must not be allowed to penetrate such a recuperative resort, else why own it? Whites cannot completely shut "them" out in the scramble for livelihood, but in their attempt to do so they cannot possibly understand the mysterious aspirations and aggressions which make a black face appear in their inviolable neighborhood, which keep the newspapers full of "their" unrest and viciousness, which prompt "them" to burn down the very houses where they live. Who can comprehend the barbaric detachment of Newark and Detroit and the rootless unconcern for home and belongings, however tenuously held?

The dismal package of black slum-life cannot be analyzed except in terms that are as imprisoning as their realities: It is black and therefore hated; it is hated and therefore poor; it is poor and therefore maleducated and slum-housed; it is maleducated and slum-housed because it is black. Life is a treadmill for blacks which permits no stopping or getting off, only a faster and more furious running. And if the treadmill smokes with friction and groans with overloading, it is because it is beginning to break down, because there is no sign of conversion in those who operate the treadmill.

The terrible pathology of racism becomes quite evident when one considers its enormous human and material cost. Slavery was introduced into America for exclusively economic reasons, with Christian morality adjusted to condone and support it. When emancipation came through the Civil War, what passed as morality would not allow freedom for slaveholders, who could not in turn allow freedom for their former slaves. In a word, slavery had quietly demanded a humanly destructive price; and a legal act like emancipation would not stop the payments. America is still meeting them.

A new phase of slavery therefore began, and slowly all of America adjusted to it, both South and North. Discrimination replaced bondage; blacks became a different kind of economic asset, a new and more or less profitable edition of "black gold." Private economy replaced the plantation as a new vehicle of exploitation; poverty replaced the slave compound as a new prop to America's private economy. *Slave* and *slavery* dropped from polite terminology and became translated into cheap labor; victim of exorbitant rents, credit, and food; customer for alcohol, narcotics, and numbers; barter in prostitution; dupe whom the law of the whites suppressed in order that their own value might continue—so do blacks enrich whites by being black.

Yet private gain in no way matches public cost. America pays conservatively fifty billion dollars annually for the extravagance of rejecting blacks. We spend five billion dollars a year for welfare, disproportionate sums of which go to black ghettos; we invest huge amounts in added police and fire protection; we sacrifice thirty billion dollars yearly because of employment bias; we suffer riot damage in the billions; we accept educational costs that under segregation in the South and comparable devices in the North go far and beyond the price of an open system, with a net product of inferior education for both whites and blacks. Beyond such prodigal and absurd waste, who can calculate what our nation loses in the stripped potential of an entire people who, whether bourgeoisie or slum dwellers, have their creativity smothered by obsequiousness or rage? Who can truly calculate what America pays for the racism of its white majority, a sickness that is an illustration of both our power and our powerlessness, a sickness that has invaded the very fiber of our lives and which permeates not only city life but international life? Beyond all doubt, whites are human or inhuman in relation to their attitude to blacks. America is what it is to its black people, and it may be a lesson that we have no time to learn.

Yet the signs of the times seldom penetrate, even if the signs are major economic crisis among blacks, urban carnage and destruction, the meaning behind the fierce talk of Stokely Carmichael and H. Rap Brown, the racist elements inherent in our Vietnam adventure, our fear and hatred of China. Apparently, white America is content to sentence itself to moral rot by reacting to black despair with measures likened by many to a fair attempt at extermination. Apparently, white America would rather see its cities burned down than rebuilt and integrated. Apparently, white America thinks it ultimately cheaper to hire more police, to call out the National Guard and the Army, than to purge itself of discrimination. Apparently, white America suspects (with profound uneasiness) that its only remaining resource against blacks is force.

There is still another sign that should clarify not only the fact of racism but its ambiguity as well. We treasure blacks in war time, though we refuse them a human life in peacetime. From time to time Americans will boast of "color-blind democracy" in the armed services while missing entirely the tragic revelation implicit in their pride: The military alone, of all American institutions, can afford the *fact* of equality. Perhaps the pride is justifiable, since we have so little other racial justice to claim. We have at least come to the point of seeing that skill in killing, or exposure to being killed, makes a man's blackness or whiteness irrelevant. Beyond that point, however, reasoning becomes infantile and vicious. We can say on the one hand that when a man kills or is killed, the experience is a man's. But we can say with even greater conviction that when a man lives, works, eats, and makes love, he does these things as a "nigger" or as a white man.

Even more significant than the irony of military integration is black participation in the Vietnam war. One can give another credit for honest confusion over Vietnam, but it is quite a different thing for another to condone the injustice of black involvement in Southeast Asia. A study by Charles C. Moskos, Jr., published by the University of Chicago's Center for Organization Studies in 1966,[3] verifies what many have long suspected: Blacks are derailed to the armed forces in disproportionate numbers because of poverty and inferior education. In civilian life black men go where they can, to the ranks of unskilled workers; in the armed forces a parallel route is taken, to combat troops. If we disregard for a moment Pentagon statistics on the subject, the percentage of black troops in combat arms has risen from 12.1 per cent in 1945 to 33.4 per cent in 1962. In all likelihood these percentages are higher today. In a word, economic and cultural deprivation makes black youngsters fit applicants for cannon fodder, a condition worsened by the extra pay and prestige given to specialized battle troops. Although blacks are about one-tenth of our national population, black dead and wounded in Vietnam are not one-tenth of the casualties—they are close to one-third.

Some interesting phenomena are already occurring in America; others are obviously in store for us. For one thing, we can no longer escape the consequences of our violence—men will no longer endure it. Our black citizens will no longer endure it; neither will the Vietnamese. And to see both tiny and very nearly powerless minorities withstand and stalemate the greatest power in history is to invite reflection on truths that we have forgotten or never learned: the invincible spirit of man, the primacy of world revolution in human rights, the limitations and weakness of power politics.

Another point, the relationship between domestic and foreign policies, must be seen as stemming from the same perverted vision of man. Thus, if we were a people of justice at home, it would be literally impossible to conceive some of our more shameful aspects of foreign diplomacy, including forms of economic imperialism, armed intervention, and overkill threat. This is not necessarily a new reality, though it may be a new lesson. America's justice in the corners of the world has always matched its justice in its own back yard. Exclusiveness at home has always been expansionism abroad, at least since we became the world's greatest manufacturing center. The question therefore remains— and it rankles deeply enough to be unavoidable—Can white America control with force both a revolution at home and one abroad (Vietnam)? And after Vietnam can it control revolutions in other countries like it, or control perhaps a whole continent in revolution? And can it do all this while trying to avoid World War III?

Let us imagine that Shylock, who in the third act of the *Merchant of Venice* rails at his persecutors—in particular Antonio, who symbolizes the malice of Christians—is a Negro. Let *Negro* therefore stand for *Jew* in the text, and let *white* stand for *Christian*. "Antonio," Shylock says, "has disgraced me and hindered me half a million, laughed at my losses, mocked at my gains, scorned my nation, thwarted my bargains, cooled my friends, heated my enemies; and what's his reason? I am a Negro. Has not a Negro eyes? Has not a Negro hands, organs, dimensions, senses, affections, passions? fed with the same food, hurt with the same weapons, subject to the same diseases, healed by the same means, warmed and cooled by the same winter and summer, as a white is? If you prick us, do we not bleed? If you tickle us, do we not laugh? If you poison us, do we not die? And if you wrong us, shall we not revenge? If we are like you in the rest, we will resemble you in that. If a Negro wrong a white, what is his humility? Revenge. If a white wrong a Negro, what should his sufferance be by white example? Why, revenge! The villainy you teach me I will execute; and it shall go hard, but I will better the instruction" (Act III, Scene 1).

Will we force blacks to "better the instruction?" It is only realistic to understand that time is short, that hate is shutting the door upon solutions, that world events are moving relentlessly to a horrible climax. One editorial dealt with the critical urgency of the situation in these terms:

The time is coming when we will regret the billions spent in Vietnam. The time is coming when we may regret the number of Negroes we have trained there in guerilla war. There is hardly a city where Negroes do not already dominate the strategic areas through which the affluent commuter passes on his way to the inner core. We cannot rebuild the sense of community so essential to our beloved country's future by engaging in a white man's war in Asia while a black man's revolt rises at home.[4]

There comes a time for candor, or for attempts in that direction. The attempts at candor registered here will necessarily flow more from the black situation than from the white, since I believe that one must speak from the lot of the oppressed rather than from that of the oppressor, the former being the issue.

Black leaders of any perception and militancy look toward white America's efforts for and against them, and conclude:

1. Selective Service is the worst current kind of racist pattern, in that it forces ghetto communities to furnish disproportionate numbers of troops for Vietnam while it extracts the best potential ghetto leadership.

THE FIRE THIS TIME?

2. The War on Poverty has little or nothing to do with poverty. It is actually a huge diversionary action to distract attention from the problem of affluence. Since the rich can hardly be expected to prevent a revolution of the poor by sharing their wealth, they subvert it before it can mobilize—by fanfare, by tolerating local political control, by hiring out black leadership, and so forth.

3. Urban renewal and the Demonstration Cities Act do more harm than good to the cause of black poor people. As practical measures, they are too limited to affect the crisis in black housing, and what is initiated tends to break up black communities and black political power.

4. Unemployment and cybernation will make blacks more and more dependent on public assistance. Economic factors maintain almost absolute control over black lives: If one works, the threatened loss of a job will keep him from militancy; if one does not work, the threatened loss of public welfare will accomplish the same end.

Without a doubt, black realization grows that white supremacy, white wealth, and white power are in effect elements of domination, and that whites have no serious intention of relinquishing status or the power that secures it. Since, on the other hand, black men are psychologically incapable of further tolerating racial subordination and powerlessness, conflict is inevitable.

Let it be made clear that what blacks do within the conflict is conditional. It is quite fully dependent upon what whites do. And blacks believe they know what we will do or not do; their experience with us has been long and unvarying, giving rise to the conviction that what we say has often little connection with what we do. In short, blacks believe the worst and expect the least—anything better will be won through struggle alone. This leaves us with several options.

One option is to establish officially what is in fact an unofficial reality—the colonial status of black America.[5] That is to say, we ought to be candid with what we have been unashamedly doing to blacks for years (as white South Africans are honest about *apartheid*, or Mississippians are honest about segregation). What is *de facto* the case—the colonization of blacks—should be legiti-

mized by law, an immensely more honest policy than the present
one, which we have honored in the breach for nearly four centuries.

As a model, the United States could take the British colonial
system at its enlightened best, but improving upon its infirmities.
Any area having over twenty-five thousand people, 75 per cent of
whom are black, could qualify as a colony. (Most major-city
ghettos would immediately meet this standard.) To protect their
interests, colonies would be represented in Washington by a
Federal department headed by a minister of Cabinet rank. They
would rule themselves, following a republican form of government, and all their laws would be valid except those in opposition
to local or Constitutional law. No black ghetto would be coerced
into becoming a colony, though it could be presumed that most
ghettos would welcome the opportunity for such a choice. Black
colonists would be obligated to pay no taxes other than those
needed for their own area; any larger services from the city, state,
or Federal governments could fall under contract. By the same
justice, colonists would not be subject to military conscription but
would control the conditions under which they would accept
military service, if at all.

Since the whole nation is responsible for the black presence and
black deprivation, some provision would have to be made for
financial support until the colonies became economically sufficient.
Twenty billion dollars annually might provide a realistic beginning, a sum that could be distributed as personal income to those
blacks afflicted by poverty. If such expenditures should cause outcries of alarm from whites one could remind them that America
is already paying more than this for its present rejection of black
people. Moreover, whites should accept with relish the fact that
subsidized black colonies would, in one fell swoop, dispel the
nagging burden of a conscience caught between its own morality
and black turbulence. In a word, both business sense and otherwise unresolvable guilt suggest that black colonies are indeed an
economy measure.

Another option would confront black rebellion with intensified legal, police, and military suppression. Under this option, any uprising by blacks would be dealt with primarily as a military problem, for which legal sanction could easily be obtained. Dixiecrats, conservative Republicans, some lobbyists, and hate and vigilante groups would favor such measures, since they believe that white crime against blacks is not the issue, but that black rebellion is. In effect, such groups believe that blacks must be forced to realize that riot and rebellion are more expensive than the despair they now live in. This thrusts the question very neatly at blacks: Submit or perish. I recall a Boston cabdriver saying substantially the same thing to me following the 1967 riots: "Let them try coming out of Roxbury, and we'll shoot the black bastards like flies. We've been looking for a chance all along."

To those who shrink from such possibilities with incredulity, with an "it could never happen in America" attitude, some reflections are offered. With hot and cold wars to "protect our interests," with our nation's commitment to overseas profits, with a cancer like racism at its very heart, with violence (injustice) permeating its domestic and international life, what are our choices? Can we do other than enlarge our grim record against black people? If it is true that Vietnam has sapped our moral and intellectual resources, is it not equally true that Vietnam is foreign fruit from the domestic vine? Who is to deny that a fearful inbreeding is going on from both sides of both oceans, with a gestation apt to result in yet more terrible progeny?

If one can imagine what is at this point the likelihood—a vicious parody of action and reaction between black and white, a vendetta whose precise aim is to do the "other" one better—one can then see that for blacks this can mean only the destruction of the sources of humiliation, and that for whites it can mean only the crushing of blacks. In all probability, therefore, the riots will continue and will slowly spread to a year-round exercise of frustration and rage. To meet them in scale, antiriot legislation will be enacted; police forces will be beefed up; the National Guard will be expanded, better trained, and mutually supported; Federal troops will be on standby more and more often. Under such counterforce black organization will stiffen, and the focus of rebellion will switch from ghetto destruction to attacks upon white business-cores, upon downtown white apartment-developments, upon white suburbs themselves. Sometime during the bitter escalation white presence and service in the ghetto will cease, putting it in a state of virtual siege. Such a tragic debacle bears many similarities to guerrilla war—indeed, blacks will say it is precisely this.

In addition, the ominous reality of detention camps will intrude once the pacification of blacks fails through lesser measures. The law now provides for a repetition of the precedent of Japanese detention during World War II, for though President Truman vetoed the McCarren Act in 1950, Congress submitted to the patriotic anxiety induced by the cold and Korean wars and passed it anyway. Title II of the McCarren Act (the Emergency Detention Section) empowers the Attorney General to apprehend and detain "in such places of detention as may be provided by him . . . all such persons as to whom there is reasonable ground to believe that such persons probably will engage in or probably will conspire with others to engage in acts of espionage and sabotage." It is clear that the President could invoke Title II following the declaration of "an internal security emergency"—namely, an invasion of the United States or its possessions, a declaration of war by Congress, or an "insurrection" within the United States in aid of a foreign enemy.

There is no discounting the availability of detention-camp sites. Such a fact has been bandied about by black leaders like Carmichael, Brown, and Floyd McKissick and by white radicals. Some of the camps have classifications of "immediate standby"; others, "sites maintained"; others, "available." Opinions regarding their capacity range from twenty to thirty thousand; but capacity is not a problem, for in the event that present accommodations become strained, others could be made quickly available. Whatever the case, it is certain that dossiers are meticulously kept on every black and white militant, and presumably, warrants for arrest are readily available. It is foreseeable, therefore, that if black rioting remains persistent, attempts will be made to pluck

out the leadership; black militants could be incarcerated and im-
mobilized at the camps for the "duration."

In a worse event, or even as a concurrent measure with the
use of detention camps, steps would be taken to protect white
homes and interests from black attack, although only listless attempts would be made to save innocent blacks from white-
vigilante retaliation. Understandably, such measures would require
an operation immeasurably more complex than the camps for
black revolutionaries. Smaller ghettos (under twenty-five thousand?) would be controlled, for example, by a pass system, cur-
few, and heavy police-guard. Larger ghettos would be reduced
to a manageable size by the massive relocation of blacks in rural
reservations. Once again, the national good would be advanced
as the rationale for the temporary suspension of black rights.

There are other options, of course, but they will remain options
and not solutions until we conceive them in justice and apply
them impartially to citizens and foreigners alike. Only a unique
and entirely unprecedented movement of justice will give Americans moral and political freedom; only justice will free those now
oppressed. Do Americans want moral and political freedom? They
do not have it now, and many will never desire it. What they now
call moral freedom is actually only an addiction to rote worship
and a vague moralism about "getting along" which are broken
without conscience when it suits them. What they now call political freedom is actually only election-day duty, which empowers
them to choose one party no worse than the other.

If Americans want something better than this, and if they want
at the same time a say and a part in the future of man, they
must renounce their slavish attachment to modes and measures of
injustice: their wealth, power, culture, morality—perhaps even
their awestruck worship of the reigning god of Westernism, technology.[6]

American wealth: There is nothing wrong about wealth, but
there is something very wrong about being wealthy while others
starve and about building wealth from the uncomprehending suffering of children, from the stagnant idleness of unemployed men,

from black skin and foreign powerlessness, from the threat or use
of arms against protest and the yearning for independence.
Wealth is very nearly America's basic hang-up. Just as greed drove
Americans to steal this land, to build it with black slaves and
colored labor, to found its empire with Yankee shrewdness and
military power, so now it impels us singlemindedly to make the
world safe for American business.

American power: There is nothing wrong with power, but there
is something very wrong when power becomes the unqualified
servant of wealth; when it completely controls politics, planning,
management, and policy; when it degenerates so easily into
weaponry and military intervention; when it ignores the powerless
and makes the powerful omnipotent; when it becomes, in effect,
a burglar alarm for the dollar. Americans need to feel what it is
to be powerless; we need to stop talking about the responsibilities
of power; we need to experience what it means to give power
away and to discover in its stead something infinitely more powerful—identity with other men and trust in them.

American culture: There is nothing wrong with our culture, but
there is something very wrong about the way we counterfeit and
abuse it. It is ostensibly Judeo-Christian, but it is really a syncretism of fealties to wealth, power, privilege, and diversified
sensuality. While Americans mimic a show of fidelity to their culture and its roots—whether Covenant or Christ, law or human
rights—they live a sophisticated kind of barbarism whose genteel
veneer is easily shattered by a black face in their neighborhood,
by a drop in the stock market, by another Communist "take-over."
Renouncing our culture would be a gain in this respect: It would
free us from the moral schizophrenia in which we now live, and
in the process free us to be the barbarians we now are.

American morality: There is nothing wrong with our morality,
but there is something monstrously evil about the way we pro-
stitute it, then defend the prostitution in the name of Christ. The
ancient Pharisees would sit at our feet with rapt attention and
relish, delighted that their ambiguity had created an historical
model. To suppose, after history's record of our aptitude for inter-

national robbery, rape, and slaughter, that our nation possesses a singular mission of dictating norms of human behavior is to merit the derision and contempt of all men. Perhaps if we divest ourselves of our morality, we will also divest ourselves of the self-righteousness employed in defending its abuse.

American technology: There is, finally, nothing wrong with technology, but there is something very wrong when technology becomes the technical machinery for profit motivation, and the international defense-envelope around profit production. Technology can make realizable the control of environment so that man might focus upon community and its formation; but using technology to stuff an already surfeited society with frills, gadgets, and images, to stimulate national fervor by moon flights and space exploration, or to mass-produce the instruments of death is not merely morally reprehensible, it is insane. And such insanity is not considered any more dispensable than the vicious nonsense it produces; neither insanity nor nonsensical hardware is easily gotten rid of. Let no one imagine, therefore, that Americans will learn that they *must* learn about human relations (or about a just application of technological science) without renouncing their apotheosis of technology.

Whitney Young of the National Urban League has called the Negro "a barometer of all America's institutions and values." He adds that the Negro "is a test of whether or not the free-enterprise system really works." [7] Mr. Young speaks with the curious faith of an establishment man; his implication is that American free enterprise *can* work for blacks, just as it *is* working for whites. The fact is that it works for neither in any viable human sense. The very condition of black people offers incontestable evidence of how it has destroyed whites.

There is nothing America fears more than revolution, wherever it might be, though our fear of it at home is undoubtedly more pronounced. And yet we cannot run from it any more than we can run from our history; the chickens have roosted, and their perch is a solid one. And it is not that the complex of institutions, customs, mores, and mythologies comprising our "way of life" is more corrupt than in the past. The corruption is merely intensified and made more glaringly evident by a nonwhite humanity that rightly regards the complex as the source of humiliation and needless suffering. In short, worldwide awareness has shaped a new man— the awareness of oppression's source has made oppression intolerable.

The mills of justice grind slowly, but they grind. If it is utopian to call upon America to reaffirm for all men the creed upon which it is founded, it is also utopian to think we can avoid the shameful fate reserved for history's empires. And it is also utopian to think we can avoid World War III.

IV

Imperialism, the Golden Rule of Peace

~~~~~~

Yes, war did come, despite the trade agreements. But it is a fact that war did not break out between the United States and any country with which we had been able to negotiate a trade agreement. It is also a fact that, with very few exceptions, the countries with which we signed trade agreements joined together in resisting the Axis. The political line-up followed the economic line-up.
— CORDELL HULL, 1948 [1]

CAPITOL CORRESPONDENTS NEVER ENTIRELY lose their humor, despite their constant contact with the grim manipulation of reality which passes for Washington politics. Some time ago a group of them devised an "LBJ Credibility Test." It was applied in this fashion: "When the President smoothes down the hair on the back of his head, he's telling the truth; when he scratches the side of his nose, he's telling the truth; when he rubs his hands together, he's telling the truth; but when he starts moving his lips, he's lying." Some other press humorists sardonically described the old Chesapeake and Ohio Barge Canal, which runs from Washington to the mountains of Maryland, as "bounded by the Cumberland Gap on the one end and the Credibility Gap on the other." [2]

Seldom has public confidence in the credibility of the Government dipped so low as it has in our time; seldom have so many Americans felt helpless with uneasy doubt. On occasion, it appears that official spokesmen make calculated efforts to deceive reporters and the public. In the recent past no issue or circumstance seemed immune from violation, whether it was the Vietnam stalemate or a weekend at the LBJ Ranch. Polls as far back as the fall of 1965 amply illustrated the destruction of trust: 67 per cent of Americans believed their Government only sometimes told the truth about Vietnam, and 13 per cent thought Washington was almost never truthful.[3]

With solid reason, one can conclude that truth has become a cold-war casualty. U Thant's famous remark rings pointedly true —the first casualty in wartime is truth—and the cold war is war. It is economic war in essence and ideological war in rationalization, with nuclear diplomacy as the substitute for political rationality.

In a real sense superpowers cannot tell the truth, and it is doubtful that they would be superpowers if they did. Cold wars have a habit of subjecting human values to cold-war values, world interests to superpower interests. Deception on any level tends to make the next lie easier. If violence begets violence, then falsehood begets falsehood; both are species of injustice, and both noisily propagate themselves.

Without question, our leaders believe their own propaganda in all sincerity—they must believe it or risk becoming schizoid. Moreover, elective office makes them captive to national mythologies, to power designs, to past mistakes, and to habits of political survival. Also, they can always escape from charges of falsehood and blunder by retreating into ideology. For example, Washington has cause to be grateful to a man like C. L. Sulzberger, who sees the Chinese engaging in a ten-year program of imperial expansion even at the cost of World War III.[4]

All this supports the fact that international power-politics, whether emanating from the Communist world or from the West, cannot be defended very well by truth. *Realpolitik* and its nation-state machinations must be kept hidden from public scrutiny, which at the least would have a tempering effect upon its immorality, and which at best would force a more upright policy. Men of power must therefore devise a new version of reality for popular consumption. They must pander to fear, horror, greed, and insecurity—they must propagandize.

An excellent illustration of the process is our quagmire in Vietnam. How often men of conscience have been revolted by the flood of deceit coming from official quarters, until they wonder wildly if the unreality communicated might not just be reality. It is not only the Government that sponsors the duplicity, it is an interest-laden complicity of all the major institutions of American life—business, church, communications media, education—all of which reach a consensus that profit, survival, and expansion lie within support of the Government's aims. It is war profiteering by Dow Chemical and Lockheed Aircraft; it is war sermons from Archbishop Robert Lucey, Billy Graham, and the late Cardinal Spellman; it is major newspapers and communications media acting out the role of an establishment press; it is chemical- and biological-warfare research at the University of Pennsylvania. It is in effect a power complex of unlimited ingenuity and resources, operating under the premises that American power can eventually fashion a Great Society of the world and thereby destroy international Communism and secure the peace. And if such convictions must sometimes compromise truth, or at other times destroy it, that is merely to concede that these convictions are more valuable than truth.

Yet shame matches incredulity among Americans in the face of their Government's breach of truth, and there is no little public resentment and anger. One might judge this as an intensifying of conscience and be grateful for it, or one might trace it to the bitter frustration resulting from the impotence of our armed might in Vietnam. Would equal outrage exist if butter were flowing at home, and if America were able to force an unconditional

surrender in Vietnam? Under such circumstances our moral disaster in Vietnam would be more monumental than at present,
since butter for the ghetto would only cool its rage, and victory
in Vietnam would decimate the peace movement.

These are sobering considerations. Conscience, like public
opinion, must be informed, or it increases confusion and helplessness. Without doubt, a vast measure of civilian repugnance to the
war is traceable to the feeling that the Administration is botching
its quarrel with the Communists and is not winning quickly, pain-
lessly, and decisively. The question of justice to the Vietnamese
is hardly a consideration, just as justice to the ghetto is hardly a
consideration. For the American way implies that if the national
purpose dictates colonialism at home or abroad, the unpardonable
sin is making a botch of the effort.

Americans of this ilk should therefore curb their anxiety over
the credibility gap and build the national "unity" required by the
Administration. If they are fervent anti-Communists (most capitalists are), why quarrel with a fervently anti-Communist government? If they are racists, why impugn Washington's racism? If
they see naked force as an answer to oppressed and outraged
human beings, what is wrong with a police state? If they live a
lie, why shouldn't their representatives lie? Political sanction for
the ruinous course of our domestic and foreign policy has been
widespread and sustained; our political representation has been
more accurate than we think.

Moreover, Congressional doves share in the naïveté of many
citizens. To an extent, the lawmakers also share in the general reluctance to go beyond a mere show of justice. As legislators, they
must of course yield before parliamentary processes, ill-informed
and sometimes hostile constituencies, and even the possibility of
political suicide. But these considerations must be balanced in
turn by the absolutely unprecedented scale of the human-rights
revolution among the world's poor, by the nature of the American
counterrevolution, and by the real good of this country and of all
humanity. It would be very hard to prove that any of the Congressional doves have made the latter considerations their real priorities. They have rather been content to attack American cold-war

policy (including Vietnam) as devious, shortsighted, brutal, and destructive of national interests. There does not seem to have been any charges from them of genocide against the Vietnamese people, of war-making as an inevitable component of liberal capitalism, of imperialism as the outgrowth of an expansionist economy. None of them have called for a completely unilateral withdrawal from Vietnam.

No one will deny the controversial character of these questions; at the same time, their obfuscation or neglect is a disservice to the true interests of humanity and accelerates the alarming slide toward World War III.

Injustice is no less unjust for one's country having performed it. If America's injustice in Vietnam is hardly debatable, and if our failure there is a direct consequence of that injustice, it serves little to express chagrin over Washington's refusal to tell the truth. "Secretary Rusk is no dope; why does he keep saying this?" [5] Of infinitely greater import are the reasons why the Administration can't—or at the very least, won't—tell the truth.

Why indeed? Lyndon Johnson is no "dope," neither is Clark Clifford, nor Walt Whitman Rostow, nor William Bundy, nor Senators like Richard Russell, John Stennis, and Everett Dirksen, nor the militarists in the Pentagon. However one might regard them, they are neither stupid nor conspiratorial. They merely operate from a combination of national interest and available power—a combination that becomes their morality. Such an exercise of morality—or power—imposes its own limits upon both policy-maker and policy, making frequent liars of the first and moral disasters of the second.

Obviously, the Administration's value system is identical with the national purpose. When this purpose is brought face to face with that of another nation, or when the Administration rationalizes this purpose before the American public, our policy-makers speak and maneuver more from imperial aim than to the realities of international relations. In the face of their stubborn and uninhibited dedication, it is thus not enough to say that they do violence to the truth, that only chauvinists and red-hunters now believe them, and that the credibility gap was a world phenomenon

before it became an American one. Our leaders are Americans to
the core and intelligent, skilled public servants, and the rationale
they advance to justify America's presence in the atrocious Vietnam war can only be the rationale of men desperately involved in
something more mysterious than their own propaganda. The
reality they seek to conceal is worse; it is so bad, in fact, that it
can seldom be offered for general consumption.

The reality is our economy and its nature. It is perhaps no
exaggeration to claim that nothing fashions us as Americans as
does our economy. It is the cornerstone upon which our mythology, folklore, history, art, and morality have been built. Americans
are par excellence the world's economic professionals; we celebrate
as does no other people the joys of wringing profit from a reluctant
creation.

As an offspring of Europe, and especially of Great Britain,
America became the logical heir to the European continent's industrial mercantilism. Our Founding Fathers were nearly without
exception affluent establishment figures—planters, tradesmen,
bankers, shippers—predominantly conservative types. Interestingly
enough, what made them conservative in their personal affairs
also made them revolutionaries toward the mother country, simply
because they would not tolerate foreign control of their businesses.
Better than the British, they saw the riches of this continent lying
fallow before them, riches they desired with no interference from
abroad. Thomas Paine's early perception of this made him a revolutionary spokesman, and in *Common Sense* (1776) he clearly
identified the issue between Britain and America as an economic
one:

'Tis not in the power of Britain to do this continent justice; the business
of it will soon be too weighty and intricate to be managed with any
tolerable degree of convenience by a power so distant from us. . . . I
have heard it asserted by some that, as America has flourished under
her former connection with Great Britain, the same connection is necessary towards her future happiness. . . . I answer roundly that America
would have flourished as much, and probably more, had no European
power taken any notice of her. The commerce by which she hath en-
riched herself are the necessities of life, and will always have a market
while eating is the custom of Europe.

Admittedly, in another context Paine, the Adamses, and Thomas Jefferson spoke precisely about personal freedom from Britain or slavery to her, for flagrant violations of human rights were very much the core of their resentments. Yet the liberty that pervaded their stirring rhetoric was nonetheless the classical American definition of liberty: the freedom to conduct national business as they thought best. It was a right associated with their handling of concrete realities like land, commodities, money, and the stuff of trade. These more than any other factors made revolutionaries out of loyal supporters of King George, and these revolutionaries supplied (they unknowing and we uncomfortable) the prototype of modern revolution.

Later on, the Louisiana Purchase did more than record a stage of territorial growth—it solidified the theme of economic expansion originally put forward by our Revolution. While solving one problem, sufficient land space for an economy of free farmers, it created another, new markets to relieve the economy of its added products. Already we had begun to overproduce. Overproduction meant markets, and markets meant that foreign expansion must follow continental expansion. Markets also meant a navy worthy of the name. Jefferson, for one, was torn between the aggressively westward land hunger and the naval power necessary to keep the high seas free and our markets open. At any rate he was the last President to hope that America could exploit a continent of such immense resources as ours while still remaining righteously isolated and thus uncontaminated by foreign intrigue.

The rush westward was, in its own time, an end in itself—it had no conscious imperial ambition about it. Our glorified pioneer forefathers had little time except to push back the frontier, shoot Indians, and settle on "free" (Indian) land. Their motivation, however, made implicit and inevitable the expansion that was to come later, since their ethic contained the working proposition, "That which can be taken, belongs."

Under this admirable rule, driving Indians off their lands, penning them in reservations, and slaughtering them relentlessly were all moral acts. The acts were moral because the Indians were immoral: They protected their land, and they resisted. Moreover, who at that stage would foolishly grant Indians the democratic prerogatives of equal time, equal representation, or equal history? They were powerless and must take the consequences.

Not to be deterred, we pushed confidently on. We had lofty ambitions in Canada, as the War of 1812 proved; though we failed in that regard, the war had beneficial side effects: It opened shipping routes to the sea and guaranteed our claims to the land west of the great trade-artery of the Mississippi. In 1819 we added Florida, and by the 1850's we had robbed Mexico of a huge northern slice of its territory and had secured the Oregon country. Finally, the Civil War came; it was at heart a traumatic dispute between the industrial and agrarian halves of the nation as to what course the new West would take, and even more importantly, as to who would run the country.[6]

In a remarkable show of commercial vision, Secretary of State Henry Clay realized as early as 1825 that the Panama Canal would be a trade convenience simplifying Atlantic and Pacific commerce. The Ostend Manifesto (1854) not only displayed our lively grasp of the harder facts of capitalistic economics, but it couched this awareness in chauvinistic and racist bombast worthy of our present anti-Communist anxieties. The Manifesto recommended that the United States take immediate steps to acquire Cuba from Spain by purchase or, failing that, by force, since, as the Manifesto said, Cuba was

as necessary to the North American republic as any of its present members. . . . We should . . . be recreant in our duty, be unworthy of our gallant forefathers, and commit base treason against our posterity, should we permit Cuba to be Africanized and become a second Santo Domingo with all its attendant horrors to the white race, and suffer the flames to extend to our own neighboring shores, seriously to endanger or actually consume the fair fabric of our Union.

At the turn of the century, when we finally went to war with Spain over Cuba and the Philippines, we abandoned the nonsense about racial mongrelization and admitted through President Grover Cleveland that the adventure was protection for our 100-million-dollar annual trade with Cuba.[7]

Conventional historical arguments about national isolationism are closer to delusion than to fact; they are the products of a tendency to write history from the compulsions of national interest. From our earliest days American diplomacy responded to American commercialism with total sensitivity, and though our entrance into European power-squabbles was restrained and prudent, we were always involved. John Jay's Treaty of 1794 very nearly made a political martyr of George Washington, because mercantile interests feared it gave undue concessions to British competitors. The Monroe Doctrine of 1823, a nationalistically slanted version of the later "sphere of influence" concept, insured our control of Latin America by indirectly demanding for ourselves what we had no intention of granting to others. The Open Door policy came later as a development of the Monroe Doctrine.

As the central theme of American history, internal development meant external expansion; disappearing frontiers at home meant an onslaught upon frontiers overseas. The republic was born in an age of empires, and there was nothing in the national consciousness to discourage the building of our own. By 1850 influential American businessmen wanted Formosa annexed, and we had made notable investment incursions in both Korea and Japan. This whetted national appetites for more, and we jealously watched (but not for long) while European powers began to parcel up China.

The evidence strongly suggests that historical Western expansion into weak (invariably colored) economies was predicated strictly on a power-weakness ratio: It went as far as resistance would allow it, and as far as profits would take it. For Western expansion into other advanced industrial nations essentially different arrangements became the rule: Economic agreements formed the basis of political alliances—either that, or war resulted. (That being the fundamental case, some interesting conjectures are in order as to what capitalist economies must become in a nuclear-armed world. Predictably enough, Western one-worlders say little of any significance about the first order of business, a basic overhaul of Western economics.)

The fact that the cross followed the flag does nothing to invalidate the auspices and aims under which America invaded the developing world. Call it naïveté or nationalism or both, but missionaries had neither the perception nor the detachment to see the game for what it was, nor to see what the Gospel ought to be in the face of it. Despite altruism and notable good will, the net effect of their efforts was to accommodate the "natives" to robbery. Behind the missionaries were the Marines; both elements had their peculiar ways of dealing with protest: the former by molding foreign Americans, the latter by threatening protest with force.

Without China—a focal point of attraction for both Europeans and ourselves—our interest in the Pacific would have been significantly less. It was, apparently, a question of vultures gathering around a corpse. That we had come late to the feast was a matter of anxious frustration; Great Britain, France, Germany, and Russia had already forced China to give them massive concessions in the form of diplomatic, trade, and military missions. True, some of our most honored pillars of society—George Cabot, George Peabody, William Sturgis, John Jacob Astor—had gained sizeable corners on Chinese silk.[8] Nevertheless, the Europeans had beaten us to the punch in carving out the more significant concessions within China.

The diplomatic equalizer intended to put us in a favorable competitive position in China was John Hay's Open Door policy. (Its ramifications have since proved to be immense, and fateful.) Regarding China, the Open Door policy intended to demonstrate that we could compete advantageously there with any or all, and that we would compensate ourselves for being dealt out of any concessions game.

Perhaps this country had no choice, or to put it more accurately, the American wielders of power had no choice (at least they apparently thought so). They apparently considered that our economic system had an inherent determinism about it, mostly because their power came from it. Senator William Frye implied as much in 1895: "We must have the market [of China], or we shall have revolution." [9] And when revolution becomes an alternative to expansion, those who fashion policy cannot be blamed overmuch for choosing expansion, particularly when they have apotheosized the system behind expansion. Furthermore, when revolution is an actual possibility, the urgency of justifying expansion can be more readily understood. Neither the system nor its momentum abroad are debatable items—it is for others to adjust to us. As Woodrow Wilson said: "Since trade ignores national boundaries and the manufacturer insists on having the world as a market, the flag of his nation must follow him, and the doors of the nations which are closed must be battered down." [10]

Senator Frye knew what he was talking about; so did President Wilson. Their concern centered on national prosperity and the necessity of sustaining it. The price of sustaining our prosperity, however, was to be paid not by this country, but by the world. In fact, the world paid the difference between our prosperity and our economic stagnation, and Americans would not have had it any other way. Our leaders proved this by their refusal to adapt or change the free-enterprise system when the masses reacted in their own way by riot and dislocation during periods of depression. It was therefore no accident that troops crushed striking Irish workers in New York City in 1846, that a depression existed both before and after the Civil War, that troops helped strikers occupy Reading and Pittsburgh during the great upheaval of 1877, that the Haymarket riot of 1886 and the Homestead strike of 1892 became landmarks of domestic violence, that the Chicago massacre grew out of the Pullman strike of 1894.

Carl Oglesby bluntly sums up the mixed character of our affluence, and the system that brings it about:

It was not silly to think that more and greater violence would come. It was not naïve to say that fundamental to the prospect of this violence was America's nagging inability to deal somehow with persistent economic and social dislocation; how to escape the boom-bust cycle, how to stabilize at a high level of employment and consumption, how to solve the problem of the concentration of power in the hands of a steadily smaller-growing cluster of men, the masters of the trusts—and how to do these things without fundamentally changing the nature of the system itself.[11]

To speak exactly, social gains for the powerless of America came about by weapons of riot and bloodshed. But such gains also swelled production costs, which could be kept competitively low only by mass production and by expanding the markets for mass produce. To this must be added the growing masses of skilled laborers and the technological strides that came from America's frequent wars. When warehouses bulged with goods and capital stagnated for want of investment, the captains of industry scoured the world for export and capital outlets while, just as feverishly, they beckoned the Government to their aid. Meantime, at home, the specter either of revolution or of basic economic instability threatened. Either event would cause an agonizing redistribution of power. Either possibility was therefore intolerable.

When prosperity seems secure, Americans celebrate its source. They exude confidence in a way of life which appears to them like the first stages of a millennium. Only in times of crisis is a profound insecurity displayed. Only then do our leaders reveal the common national doubt; they prime the economy and gloomily predict the consequences of recession. In substance, they tell us that America must oil, improve, and enlarge its economic machinery to produce more, for more production means a rising saturation point of consumption, and better management of the wealth and buying power of foreigners. And though this effort is made in concert with an official outcry in favor of freedom, human rights, cultural uplift, and anti-Communism, our leaders have something else in mind. Their dedication is to the American empire, to the system that supports it, to their power within it, and finally, to the fruits of empire which filter down through the public pyramid.

When lacunae in logic appear, ideology fills the gap. And Americans can be as flexible with their own ideology as they are with the ideology of others. We have, for example, proved time and again that rival ideologies are no practical threat as long as there are mutual economic ties to absorb the strain. So it is that relationships with Spain, Portugal, the Union of South Africa, Thailand, Indonesia, South Korea, and Latin dictatorships become problems of propaganda rather than of opposing value systems. Propaganda coats the realities, and it is gulped down, simply because it is in our interest to do so. At present, for instance, certain Marxist countries have become almost respectable to us. They are no longer under the Russian monolith, we are told; they are becoming capitalistic and "free." But the fact is that both we and they are willing to trade, and it is profitable to do so. In such a fashion does the "free, democratic" world conduct its business with what it used to refer to as "the Communist slave bloc."

Corporate capitalism is thus more than an attitude among Americans; it is a creed. We can forgive our leaders for being doctrinaire about it—they are merely high priests preaching the national faith. It is a faith, incidentally, which both pervades and transcends religious denominationalism, so much so that Christian or Jewish sectarianism is not as weighty a matter as well-meaning people think it to be. With a consensus approaching universality, Christian and Jew unite today in a kind of technocratic Calvinism to form the Great American Church, with its fervent synthesis of moralized economics. This, one might gather, is our national theology, and the community that springs from it has sufficient cohesion and missionary zeal to throw the traditional achievements of established religion into eclipse.

To return, however, to our history. Many consider Wilson a great President, and he may possibly be considered so, if one prepares to disregard his championing of liberal capitalism. In his Columbia University lectures of April, 1907, he said frankly: "Concessions obtained by financiers must be safeguarded by ministers of state, even if the sovereignty of unwilling nations be outraged in the process. Colonies must be obtained or planted, in order that no useful corner of the world may be overlooked or left unused." [12] In 1912 he hailed American expansionism as both fact and challenge: "Our industries have expanded to such a point that they will burst their jackets if they cannot find a free outlet to the markets of the world." [13]

Just before World War I broke out, with America in one of its periodically serious recessions, Secretary of Commerce William Redfield revealed to a convention of the National Council of Foreign Trade in May, 1914, the highly American view that economic welfare was the chief source of political welfare. "Because we are strong," he told the businessmen, "we are going out, you and I, into the markets of the world to get our share." [14] Secretary of

State William Jennings Bryan followed him to the rostrum to remind the audience that official policy was to

> open the doors of all the weaker countries to an invasion of American
> capital and enterprise . . . In Spanish-speaking countries hospitality is
> expressed by a phrase, "My house is your house." . . . I can say, not
> merely in courtesy but as a fact—my Department is your department;
> the ambassadors, the ministers, and the consuls are all yours. It is their
> business to look after your interests and to guard your rights.[15]

With an economy so insatiably aggressive, efforts by thoughtful
Americans to inquire whether running the world's business was
truly good for others or for ourselves seldom gained more than
marginal attention. As for our leaders, they apparently thought
we would muddle through, getting our way by a mixture of
divine help, raw power, bluff, and characteristic good luck. Wilson
suspected, as did many Presidents before and after him, that
America's overseas scramble for markets, aided and abetted by a
first team of diplomats and by a backup force of the Navy and
Marines (Army on occasion), would cause outrage and massive
tensions abroad. But he naïvely thought showdowns could be contained by alliances, diplomatic maneuvers, world opinion, and international tribunals. Interestingly enough, in 1912 he shared the
opinion of Elihu Root and William McKinley before him that
Germany was the most dangerous economic rival of the United
States, which certainly suggests that economic conflict was a substantial cause for our struggle with Germany in World War I.

In any event, during World War I many of the basic contradic-
tions of our foreign policy began to appear. Most of them hinged
upon what we now call self-determination, a right that is, to most
Americans, self-explanatory in its meaning and scope. At face
value, one would think that what most Americans consider the
genuine humanitarianism that has always been a part of our
foreign relationships would have actively promoted self-determination. It would have normally, were it not for two other
ingredients of our foreign policy. The first concerned our motivation in giving. We wanted others to be more American; we wanted
them, in effect, to be our cultural subjects. This all but destroyed

the ideal of self-determination. The second brought about a further deterioration of that idea: Our colonizers–diplomats, businessmen, missionaries–operated under the premise that foreign economies existed primarily to enrich America. So our foreign expansion provided the increment of profit which in fact secured our prosperity. Raymond Robins' comment on Woodrow Wilson reveals the latter as a kind of fateful prophet of America's dilemma:

Wilson was a great man, but he had one basic fault. He was willing to do anything for people except get off their backs and let them live their own lives. He would never let go until they forced him to, and then it was too late. He never seemed to understand there's a big difference between trying to save people and trying to help them. With luck you can help 'em—but they always save themselves.[16]

Obviously, the things we wanted *from* others were vastly more important to us than the things we wanted *for* them.

Our distortion of self-determination reveals not only that we are disciples of John Locke and his economic determinism, but that our foreign policy is equivalent to our dogma of the Open Door. John Hay's Open Door policy, brought to concrete expression by William McKinley, Theodore Roosevelt, and Woodrow Wilson, still defines America abroad. Roughly speaking, it gave us the assumed right to poach for foreign resources, labor, and markets without taking upon ourselves the full weight of the white man's burden. With a sophistication remarkable for a nation comparatively new at the game, we developed a kind of colonialism which got the profits out without entrapping ourselves in the European habit of occupation and control.

At the heart of such an approach was an ambiguous conception of natural law, a conception that gained justification from the harmony of interests which it supposedly brought about. In applying natural (nationalist?) law, we invariably assumed that others would profit from an invasion of their economies and their lives, and we resented their resistance as unenlightened and ungrateful. To them, our efforts were an a priori insolence; to us, they were common sense and so reasonable that they ought to be a pattern for the world. Had not similar efforts subdued a continent for us? Had they not amassed prodigious wealth and power, making

America a paradigm for the nations? To reject them out of hand was to be irrational and even "unnatural." And it is precisely this attribute of "unnaturalness" in others which invited American decisions to "help" them in spite of themselves, at the point of bayonet if necessary. Later on, at the end of a long process, they would see the wisdom of this, and then they would be rational and "natural."

Consequently, natural law as applied to our economics means what is natural (best) for us, despite what it may cost others. Notwithstanding the pure form of self-interest implicit in this, what is best for us is rigidly judged as best for others. Add to this perceptive subtlety a contempt of foreigners and their ways of life; add to it conventional American racism; and one has a national attitude of horrifying dimensions. The tragedy of this attitude would be grave enough if only we were punished by it. But we are an expansionist nation (empire), and others must suffer as well.

Our loose and rhetorical employment of self-determination relative to other nations is perhaps the best possible evidence that the dogma is in fact one of the meatier phrases of national ideology. Followed to its real consequences, true self-determination means more than allowing other nations to work for their goals at their own pace while preserving an utter respect for their culture and autonomy. It also means helping them under these strict conditions. Indeed, as William A. Williams points out, self-determination leads ultimately to international pacifism and to the guaranteed right of anarchism within smaller communities.

Such conclusions cause astonishment and anger in the halls of power, mostly because our masters have a far keener interest in manipulative power than in human rights. It has been pointed out that with this kind of overload, power is more attractive than wealth. Whatever the case, power and wealth are inextricably joined, and their combination usually militates against human rights and freedom despite righteous claims to the contrary.

Perhaps a few more instances will lend consistency and flesh to the national theme. The great crash of 1929 and the depression that followed it can be traced in no small part to the plummet of

American exports from 5 billion dollars in 1929 to 1.6 billion dollars in 1934. Roosevelt's New Deal did not intend to attack this problem structurally—it intended simply to alleviate the domestic crises of insolvency and unemployment until the revival of foreign trade became possible. Concurrent with WPA, NRA, CCC, and similar domestic measures were the Trade Agreements Act of 1934 and the repeal of the protectionist Smoot-Hawley tariffs, both aimed at restoring European ability to buy our exports.[17]

Assistant Secretary of State Francis B. Sayre soberly revealed how Washington felt about declining world trade:

What does this decrease in American trade actually mean in the lives of our farmers and manufacturers? Although it is true that the United States normally exports only about one-tenth of its total production, nevertheless, certain staples are dependent for their continued existence upon an export of very much more than one-tenth. . . . The failure to sell these surpluses abroad would mean inevitable disaster to great agricultural sections of our country. Such destitution and economic disaster would not be confined to the producers themselves. It would be transmitted through diminished purchasing power, into the business life of every town and village in the producing area, and from these would spread injury throughout our country. Without the income from the sales of these surpluses, real estate values must fall sharply, tax revenues must be curtailed, banks threatened, and the cultural life of entire sections of the country stricken, if not permanently injured. . . . Cut off these foreign markets, and the inevitable result is unemployment, suffering, and human misery.[18]

No one could have been in fuller accord than Roosevelt himself. Doing anything else would be like refusing to bow to the inevitable. In 1935 he said, "Foreign markets must be regained if America's producers are to rebuild a full and enduring domestic economy for our people. *There is no other way* [my italics] if we would avoid painful economic dislocations, social readjustments, and unemployment." [19]

There is little profit in quoting from the interim, except for President Johnson's speech to a Convention of Junior Chamber of Commerce executives in Baltimore on June 27, 1967. His remarks deserve mention, not only because they sustain an economic theme as old as America itself, but because they perfectly fit our cold-

war stance. According to him, our wealth might very well be
a temptation to other nations, which might have to be restrained
in their greed. The President reflected first on the blessings of the
private-enterprise system:

We own almost a third of the world's railroad tracks. We own almost
two-thirds of the world's automobiles—and we don't have to wait three
years to get a new one, either. . . . We own half the trucks in the world.
We own almost a half of all the radios in the world. We own a third of
all the electricity that is produced in the world. We own a fourth of all
the steel. . . . *Although we have only about 6% of the population of the
world, we have half its wealth* [my italics]. Bear in mind that the other
94% of the population would like to trade with us. Maybe a better way
of saying it would be that they would like to exchange places with us.
I would like to see them enjoy the blessings that we enjoy. But don't
you help them exchange places with us—because I don't want to be
where they are. Instead, I believe that we are generous enough—I believe that we are compassionate enough—and I believe that we are
grateful enough that we would like to see all of them enjoy the blessings
that are ours.[20]

Apparently, he knew his audience. They interrupted him re-
peatedly with applause; at the end they gave him a standing
ovation. They did what most minor capitalists would do—relish
what he said and ignore what he implied.

   Before investigating the nature of native generosity, compassion, and gratitude, we ought to look at the chief purveyor of
such virtues, the American supercorporation. These are not cartels
in the old international sense (they desire monopoly as little as
America desires territory) but rather industrial conglomerates
that incorporate the functions of research and invention, of dis-
persing capital, of management and market manipulation (advertising), all the while emphasizing a diversity of production, a
factor that helps them amass capital and power and gain flexi-
bility enough to go where the profits are, either for manufacturing or for extracting minerals and oil.
   A case in point is General Motors, which has a million and one-
third shareholders in eighty countries, plants in twenty-four

countries, and products ranging from automobiles to missile-guidance systems. General Motors' net profit of 2.1 billion dollars in 1965 was more than the general revenue of forty-eight states, and its total sales of 21 billion dollars exceeded the gross national product of all except nine foreign nations.[21] They may exceed all except seven nations now.

The Federal Government, which traditionally opposed trusts for their monopolizing tendencies, now enthusiastically supports them in their diversified form. Such empathy springs from various factors, such as the harmonious reciprocity between business and the Government (business lobby in Washington, diplomatic initiatives favoring business abroad), the reluctance to update antitrust legislation, and marked delusions by the Government as to the efficiency and overall contribution of the corporate giants. Underlying the above factors are business and the Government's identical philosophies of power, and similar commitments to the dynamics of national bureaucracies.

Industrial conglomerates are products of mergers. Over four thousand American companies disappear annually through merger, a tactic that allows two hundred corporations to control 60 per cent of America's manufacturing wealth and virtually all principal markets. Competition is less and less a matter of product quality; rather, quality has been relegated to Madison Avenue as its province and responsibility. Products therefore tend to have standard costs through coordinated pricing, overdesign, garish packaging, inferior performance or quality. Comparable models from Ford, Chrysler, and General Motors are convenient examples. They differ in price by pennies or a few dollars. All have structured obsolescence; most are obscene in style and disastrous in engineering. In the last analysis, it is simply absurd to suppose that healthy competition will result from noncompetitive structuring. Again, profit is the object, not consumer satisfaction.

What do conglomerates suggest in tendency, if not in effect? They suggest a centralization in power that goes beyond themselves—a coalition of economic, political, and military interests that have achieved an astounding harmony of concern and that work with ruthless effect as a team. With war appropriations reaching inconceivable levels of federal outlay, with the gross national product depending more and more on war production, it is useless to debate whether America is now a civilian or a military economy. Apart from the professional jealousies that might be stirred, State Department cold warriors could exchange business suits for Defense Department uniforms with no loss of nationalist efficiency.

Nonetheless, in spite of the harmonious and exclusive nature of our imperial triumvirate, politicians and generals accede to the root power vested in the economic (technological) oligopolies. America is a technocracy; they know this and glory in it. And it is a fact that presents no particular problems to them. Indeed, politicians and military men need one another, but they need industrialists more. All are unequal powers on the same team, since industrialists are the quiet power behind throne and command post.

Obviously, the future holds more of the same. Power will continue to centralize (or try to), not because government tends to move toward Washington, not because "that's where the money is," but because Federal centralization serves economic centralization best. A rough outline of America today would look like this: small bureaucracies merging with other small bureaucracies to equal large bureaucracies, which merge with each each other to form summit bureaucracies, which equal what Fred J. Cook calls the warfare state.

Such phenomena are not entirely new in our history, though recent developments indicate a perilous, even irremediable, course. There has always been in America a correlation between the levels of industrial wealth and the levels of Federal bureaucracy. At any given time since our revolution the gut problem of national life has been simply this: how to get effective representation in Washington for economic power. Richard Barber implies what Washington must be as a governmental reality and what the Defense Department must be as a military reality in the following manner: "Within a decade a group of 200 American companies plus another 50 to 100 large foreign enterprises will possess most of the world's manufacturing assets and make the great preponderance of sales and profits, having as tight a grip on global industry as our big companies now have at home." [22] In the minds of our more ambitious nationalists such possibilities must cause dreams of Washington as the world's capital.

What is the chance of domestic and international justice? Where is the hope of world peace in the face of prospects like these? Chance and hope remain, that is true, and never fully disappear, but they recede far enough to become almost purely academic matters. If any one factor will save humanity from burning in its own cauldron, it is the concrete realization of human rights: the just and universal distribution of goods and liberties. Evidence suggests, however, that the world's rich have no intention of sharing wealth or allowing human liberty, for if they did, it would mean abandoning the very things that keep them what they are and where they are. They rather choose to take their chances on their own position, on the capitalism that supports it, on the naked force that defends it, and on the fog of propaganda that vainly attempts to make it rational.

One can no longer deal with desperate people as mere pockets of desperation—the world is no longer that kind of world. In a very real sense, therefore, America's poor exemplify the world's poor. Both strive to make an issue of economic inequality; both move toward revolution as a means of redress. In America eighty million people (nearly half our population) receive 17 per cent of the income, whereas ten million at the top control an almost identical amount (15 per cent).[23] However sobering, such an appraisal does nothing to illustrate the growing income-gaps between 40 million poor and 160 million middle and upper class. The futureless sterility of the poor stems from the fact that as America grows wealthier, the poor grow poorer; they do not share proportionately the increase of wealth, which in effect leaves them further behind in their helplessness and need. The rising gross national product is therefore not for all Americans. It leaves the poor constant in number and condition; they remain literally the "others" who are always with us.

When the world's poor look at all America in the same fashion that America's poor look at America's rich, three billion people see

two hundred million with the same wealth as themselves, or an
average of fifteen times as much per person. When two billion
colored people desperately subsist on one-fifth of the world's
wealth, they can one billion whites (including Russians) so
curely living on four-fifths, and busily accumulating more.

Such conditions are more than grist for war they are war, of
a cowardly and grisly kind, for which America bears outstanding
responsibility. We cannot escape judgment from such applied
horror; the judgment comes from innocent children destroyed by
intellectual genocide in our slums and from starving and hopeless
people in the developing nations. We refuse to challenge our violence because we have the power to call it something else. What
we call the violence of the poor—divisive, irresponsible, dema-
gogic, traitorous—is what we ought to call our own violence.

Perhaps the enormity of our injustice can be measured by the
lengths we go to contain the reaction to it, whether by para-
military plans for our threatened cities or by counterinsurgency
efforts abroad or by the overkill blanket, which (our leaders tell
us) protects our precious "freedoms." Perhaps the judgment of
our leaders about defense measures is entirely accurate; perhaps
an empire must have its garrison arms and propaganda. Perhaps
one injustice must be piled on another to sustain the first or to
prevent, at least temporarily, a reckoning.

The vulnerability or near helplessness of foreign economies
before our goliaths of business illustrates one paramount fact: As
capitalists, we have neither equals nor rivals. The reason is simple:
Our hearts are with our treasure, and other people will not make
the same investment of heart.

With characteristic Yankee acumen, we prefer to invest in the
more advanced industrial communities, since we esteem the advantages of political stability and steady growth over a lesser
return. It is now estimated that our total direct investments in Europe approach twenty billion dollars, and when Europe is combined with Canada, the two areas account for over 60 per cent of
all U.S. direct investments.[24] The rates of return on our European
direct investments hover consistently above domestic returns, 13
per cent against 8–10 per cent. It is little wonder under the

circumstances that Europeans use angry terms like "industrial
helotry" and "sellout," and men like President De Gaulle fear that
American business threatens the economic and political independence of European nations.

This is a mystifying matter to laymen, in light of the industrial
competence of Europeans and the control they enjoy over their
own backyard. How is it that "the aggregate sales of Volkswagen,
Fiat, Daimler-Benz, British Motors and Renault are only two-
thirds of Ford's sales, only one-third of G.M.'s"? How is it that

Americans now control 80% of Europe's computer industry, 90% of the
microcircuit industry . . . and sizable shares of chemicals, farm machinery and oil[?] In Britain, U.S. companies own half of all modern
industry, employ one of every 17 workingmen, manufacture 10% of all
British goods for some consumption or export. U.S. firms also squeeze
out twice as much profit from invested capital as their British competitors.[25]

How is it that Europeans readily admit their Common Market is
American in organization, and why do they fear that if present
trends continue, the third industrial power in the world (after
the United States and the Soviet Union) will be American industry in Europe? [26]

One reason is that multinational operations by American conglomerates allow them to sidestep the antitrust legislation of the
invaded countries. Another is even more significant—the technology gap. America invests nearly four times the amount in research and development (thirty billion dollars) than does all of
Europe (eight billion dollars), thereby giving its corporations
such an immense technological advantage that Alain Peyrefitte,
the French Science Minister, asserts that Europe risks "falling as
far behind the United States as the underdeveloped nations are
behind Europe." [27] In effect, the "technology gap" results from
our vast expenditures for military and space programs, our more
sophisticated and extensive computer technology, and the "brain
drain" that currently plagues Europe. Consequently, Europeans
find to their chagrin that they cannot compete, and more often
than not they answer by gracefully capitulating.

The annual return on American direct investments in the world

may now inch toward 14–15 per cent. Lower European profits
and those still lower on domestic levels are padded by a 62 per
cent annual profit in the Middle East, 50 per cent in Libya, 21
per cent in Peru, 18 per cent in Venezuela. The latter figures provide some index of the profitability of the developing world. American profiteers call such profits the reward of risk. But Latin
Americans, for example, prefer to judge them from the standpoint
of their own wealth and their own labor. With a little effort, one
can understand their viewpoint: "In 1956, we invested [in Latin
America] $500 million and returned a profit almost half again as
big, $770 million; for a net capital loss to Latin America of $220
million." [28]

It is a redundancy to maintain that this is the stuff of empire.
All the confused debates about isolation and isolationism are swept
away before it. Americans make four-fifths of all foreign investments today, and though their working assumptions might include
such altruisms as the internal development of other nations, the
overriding object is the lush rewards of foreign economic enterprise:

Of the 500 largest [American] corporations, 386 had notable foreign
operations. A score or two of the large companies have a third or more
of their total assets abroad; some eighty of these firms derived 25% or
more of their sales and earnings from overseas. Sales of foreign-based
U.S. manufacturing firms have increased more than five times since
1950. In 1965, it has been conservatively estimated, earnings on foreign
investments amounted to more than 20% of the after-tax profits of domestic non-financial corporations.[29]

Profits like these demand a climate—a climate that the American Government feels obligated to create. Part of the climate is
the omnipresence of the military, military intelligence, and the
CIA; part of it also is the ministrations of the Agency for International Development. Indeed, AID's role in the developing world
strenuously calls into question the real rationale behind "foreign
aid," which annually comes under violent attack in Congress and
in reactionary circles as a "giveaway program" and "sand down a
rat hole." It is hardly either. Indeed, that such an attack is maintained and treated with credibility by press and public, or that

liberals are deluded into believing that "foreign aid" is really foreign *aid*, suggests considerable design to convince the American people of the myth of their generosity in the face of an ungrateful and spiteful world. It is a myth that neatly reinforces those of Communist "conspiracy" and of our position as "sinless but sinned against."

The Agency for International Development is actually nothing more than the chief agency by which Washington finances foreign business, and under this heading it distributes about two billion dollars a year, 85 per cent of which is spent in the United States to buy goods, raw materials, and services. AID dovetails neatly with the international financial institutions dominated by America —the World Bank, the International Finance Corporation, the Export-Import Bank—all of which readily finance American corporate ventures or prepare the infrastructure (roads, railroads, docks, power development) that private capital feels ought to precede it.[30]

D. A. Fitzgerald, a former administrator of the Agency for International Development, denies the assumption that foreign aid has economic assistance as its main purpose:

A lot of the criticism of foreign aid is because the critic thought the objective was to get economic growth, and this wasn't the objective at all. . . . The objective may have been to buy a lease, or to get a favorable vote in the UN, or to keep a nation from falling apart, or to keep some country from giving the Russians airbase rights, or any one of many other reasons.[31]

Senator Wayne Morse was even more critical in 1964:

Sad to say, of the economic section of the program not more than half is devoted to bona fide economic development. Supporting assistance, the contingency fund, and nonproject loans from the development loan fund are but political props and payoff to foreign governments. They do not develop, they merely patch over and perpetuate lack of development. Even the technical assistance program is being used for transportation and communication projects against the day when they may be of use to American forces, and to train small-time police states in emerging countries.[32]

Our "gifts" to Latin America run about a billion dollars a year, most of it in low-interest loans. Many of these loans go to Latin-American subsidiaries of U.S. firms, or they are AID loans contracting for U.S. goods and services. "Seed" money of this kind results in five billion dollars in U.S. sales to Latin American countries, a shocking portion of which is for arms. (Some of the more obvious advantages of arming Latin American dictatorships with our obsolete weapons are a reduction in the balance-of-payments deficit, self-imposed policing by the countries themselves, rivalries and squabbles which keep the area beneficially [for us] weak, the maintenance of poverty, which keeps labor and raw materials cheap and deepens dependence on us.)

Under such curious aspects of "self-determination" policy, Brazil must annually devote 24.2 per cent (300 million dollars) of its export earnings to service its debts to America; Argentina, 250 million dollars; Chile, 140 million dollars. When reimbursements like these are considered in light of the fact that Latin America is the most stagnant economic area in the world, with a per capita growth rate of 1.7 per cent from 1960 to 1965, one can only conclude that Latin America is to us a mere economic colony, which we hold in an iron fist of dollar diplomacy, puppet oligarchies, and the threat of military intervention. The testimony of deed is, after all, the most weighty evidence.

As for Africa, the storm signals are out, but time alone will tell whether Africans will keep them flying. Vice-President Humphrey's nine-nation African tour at the beginning of 1968 was an attempt to pull them down with ideology and economics. Humphrey knew that the area was especially critical of America's racism and of its intervention in Vietnam. He also knew that our shattered image must be reconstructed before Africans would look favorably upon an influx of American capital. To this end, Mr. Humphrey took with him Associate Supreme Court Justice Thurgood Marshall, who publicly bemoaned that the only American Negroes Africans knew were Stokely Carmichael and H. Rap Brown. Apparently there were others, including himself, who could testify to the "progress" that American blacks had made.

It is incredibly difficult for nations who are still in preindustrial times to resist the blandishments of quick loans or quick industrial development. Nevertheless, Africans have two advantages of perspective on their side. They have had experience with European colonialism, and they are generally aware of the objectives of both American and Russian diplomacy. Consequently, they probably suspect that superpowers can be trusted only when it is in their (America's and Russia's) interest to be trusted. Proof of this is near at hand: American support of Portuguese colonialism and South African *apartheid,* plus our intervention in the Congo. Understandably, therefore, Africans are doing more looking than leaping. Their reservations toward us can perhaps be summed up by an East African Foreign Minister who talked with an American reporter as they looked out over the Indian Ocean. His country had no harbor, and he told the reporter of a proposal the United States had made him for a loan of twenty million dollars to build one. "By the the time we paid the service charges," he said ruefully, "we would have had only eight million dollars with which to actually construct the harbor."

History attests that even as wealth is the singular aim of empire, so also is it empire's tragic fault and fundamental weakness. The reason is not that complicated (it rather becomes complicated because it is so seldom accepted): Men lose human perspective through greed, and they see others as helps or hindrances to possession, not as persons like themselves.

Scripture resolutely attacks this problem, both in empires and in persons. "Empire passes from nation to nation because of injustice, arrogance, and money" (Ecclesiasticus 10:8). Christ warned that discipleship was impossible without renunciation of possession (Luke 14:33) mainly because He knew that men would not accept one another as brothers as long as wealth intervened. He stated flatly that poverty was a blessing in disguise (Luke 6:20), implying thereby that riches were a curse in disguise. James, who was the Lord's relative, reserved terrible words for the wealthy: "Now an answer for the rich. Start crying, weep for the miseries that are coming to you" (James 5:1).

At the very least, discipline toward goods removes a giant obstacle from reverence toward men. By the same token, as dedication to goods grows, so does justice in a man suffer proportion-

ately, and so does love decline and die. What can be said of people can also be said of nations—the issue is essentially the same.
America's lust for comforts finds proof in its selection of poor
(mostly blacks), its obtrusion of the poor (black or white), its refusal to do enough to solve the problem of poverty, its pollution
of the air and water, its defense (aggression?) by a conscript
army, its trust in doomsday weapons. All are justifications for extravagance and the thirst for more wealth which extravagance
brings. The empty rhetoric about justice at home and abroad is,
if anything, more common than ever, but the substance of justice
is little more than a crumbling facade. The poor everywhere see
American justice for what it is: welfare, economic exploitation,
and war.

Nor do the traditions of voluntary poverty within Roman Catholicism temper appreciably America's rapt pursuit of affluence.
In this instance, as in many others, the Gospel has been bent to fit
the impressive array of institutional benefits and professional
tastes. As a movement within the American Church, only the
Catholic Worker has accepted poverty as a requirement of the
Christian life and not as an option. The consequent freedom
gained from such an attitude has been priceless—freedom to identify militantly with men everywhere who are suffering under war,
racism, and involuntary poverty.

Generally, however, Catholics are like other Christians in
America—they are Mississippians in race relations and Calvinists
in economics. The credentials of institutional Catholicism for recognition as part of racist, affluent America are its day by day bewilderment before black pain and rage, and its assets of 44.5 billion dollars. Under the trying circumstances of our time it generally speaks only for and to itself—that is, it speaks primarily to
preserve itself. As in other power sectors of American society,
the issue is seen more and more clearly as one of survival.

But what America is, is also what America does. What we are
and what we do deserves further investigation—in the cold war,
in the matter of ABC arsenals, in Vietnam. Under such urgencies
we may understand more fully the difference between doing
justice, doing nothing, and doing what we do. Dives was buried

in hell not because he hated Lazarus or cast him from his table or set the dogs on him, but because he did nothing. We are not content with doing nothing; we bleed the poor, ignore them when they are quiet, crush them when they rise. And this may be our epitaph.

V

Cold-War Aspirations and Secrets

*Those were countries simple to observe, difficult
to interpret. Young men are sage and bearded; grandmothers
are pretty; the married care little for marriage, but have*

*many babies; black and white were never so close and cordial,
and never hated so much; elder counsellors are brainless
but play good tennis. Their heroes, who are genuine*

*heroes, are also killers. These people can do anything
difficult, but nothing easy: catch and tame sight
and sound out of space; stroll in it; fly tons of steel*

*and come down on a handkerchief, yet cannot realize a simple
covenant. Hundreds of wise men are united by subtle
communication, to form one mind and talk like a single idiot.*

*We have seen angels dropping fire on straw villages,
and fiends sentimentally entertained by pitiful
musicians imitating the entertainers of angels.*

*We have seen more good than ever we saw before
accomplishing unendurable evil.*

We have seen a whole world ruled by a handful of men.
No two from one country.
    —RICHMOND LATTIMORE, "Report from a Planet"

IN THE LULL FOLLOWING V-E DAY IN 1945, I
spent some ten days in the German city of Münster. An unthink-
ing kind of relaxation had come upon myself and the officers with
me, a relief as huge as it was unconscious. The war in Europe had
ended, and with resistance crushed and an armistice underway,
we slipped into a detachment that had little to do with the ruin
around us.

The Americans in Münster were billeted in the basement of a
partially destroyed school; the quarters were reasonably dry and
comfortable, despite the heavy spring rains. But outside, mile
upon mile of urban desert stretched over the flat Westphalian
plain. The tortured and riven buildings reminded one of scenes
in our arid Southwest, where giant internal forces had broken
and thrust up the earth's crust, only to scatter it pell-mell.

The sweet stench hanging over the city reminded us that Münster was a vast, accidental cemetery, with people rotting where
the explosives had caught them—in homes, offices, even churches.
The survivors had for the most part scattered to the countryside;
the few who remained peeked at us from burrowed-out cellars—
the children with curiosity, the women with dull, stolid hatred
(there were no men). Such must have been the gaze of conquered toward conqueror as long as men had gone to war and
done the work of war. The eyes in these faces were blue and the
hair about them blond—features that provoked clumsy references
to Hitler's insane dream of Nordic supremacy.

Out of boredom, we toured Münster daily, finding it everywhere the same. A massive abstraction had been imposed upon
the city—an abstraction beginning with the print of Allied bombing manuals and ending here with this sheer, incomprehensible
ruin. We saw not one building untouched or whole; more often
than not, their shattered walls and roofs overflowed onto the

streets. Only main thoroughfares had had the benefit of bull-
dozers. Everywhere else, bombs had torn up the streets or buried
them beneath floods of fallen masonry,

We learned that Münster was an ancient seat of Catholic solidarity, the capital of Westphalia, and a great rail center. The rail
yards had been an early and favorite target; the devastation there
had been complete and was no less grotesque. Locomotives,
coaches, boxcars and flatcars lay tossed about haphazardly amid
the twisted rails—burned, twisted, shredded—some on their sides,
others on their backs or ends. An officer with me made a wry comment: "It looks like a model-train buff's cellar after a boy-vandal
had kicked hell out of it!"

The swastika shone ominously from the wreckage. Painted on
equipment here and there in silver or white, it told us what we
could not understand then of a Christianity turned in upon itself like the limbs of a spastic, sponsoring from its perverted exclusiveness and grotesque energy an era of sustained horror:
shrieking national pride, blood racism, Junker militarism, gas-
oven genocide, a plague of fratricide let loose upon a continent.
The swastika was an apt symbol for Nazism, but nothing could
straighten its cruciform limbs but the Body no longer there.
Germans had replaced It with nothing—worse still, It had strutted
around in the little corporal from Munich, in whom they had de-
posited their idolatrous hopes. As the war proved, Hitler was history's most dangerous idol—as the agony and death of millions
proved, and as this rubble proved.

Other colleagues ranged farther afield, and one described to us,
with the florid salesmanship that Americans use to gain attention,
a bombed-out hospital. He went on in detail, worrying and relish-
ing his subject like a boy who had seen his first snake. "You
oughta see it," he exclaimed. "Terrific! They got some of them
fetuses in bottles, and a bunch of naked women lying around in
vats. Just like a museum, only better. And headquarters don't
keep guards there, so you can stay as long as you wanna. We
stayed all afternoon, didn't we, Joe?" Joe leered and winked like
a partner in conspiracy, then went on reading his GI paperback.

Being red-blooded American boys like them, with the same crudities and imperceptions, we went. We found the hospital with difficulty. It was apparently some kind of small private foundation like those commonly found in America. In all likelihood, it had been kept operating only because of terrible necessity, or it had escaped bombing until the last, total raids. Its doctors and nurses, now dead or dispersed, had known the fierce irony of their profession in war: the attempt to preserve life when destruction engulfs all the efforts to do so.

When we arrived, we saw that nothing of the hospital's exterior structure remained but a timbered entrance cut through rusty steel and heaped brick. Endless steps led us deep underground into a large laboratory room, poorly lit, uncomfortably hot, and permeated with an indescribable mixture of heavy, fetid odors. With characteristic economy, the Germans had stockpiled bodies there in the elusive hope that the dead could somehow serve the living, thereby proving that death had not been utter waste.

It was a scene defying the usual powers of description, and twenty-three years obscures my memory. The bodies were victims of bombing, and the huge room was choked with them—men, women, and children of every age—their tombs rectangular vats of formaldehyde, their nakedness displaying openly the wounds of death. For reasons of anonymity or cranial trauma all were headless, though there was a strange, collective dignity about them. One little boy, not more than nine, had his right leg excised crudely at the hip. One could imagine how he bled to death in loneliness and fatal shock.

The formaldehyde had receded from the bodies, or there had not been enough to keep them submerged. And so a grisly kind of picnic was going on: Swarms of bluebottle flies circled lazily in the heat, digesting their horrid diet in midair. Curious GI's kept them from alighting again to the banquet, but while forced to wait, they could breed and defecate. They had a kind of over-fed patience about them—eventually, the visitors would leave.

We could not comprehend then, or even now, what all that

meant: the ravaged city, its dead and refugee population, its em-
balmed victims in that stinking cellar. In a civilized world Münster alone would be assault enough upon conscience, rent enough
in the social fabric, testimony enough of the barbarian lurking
just below the surface in all of us. But the war had multiplied
Münster two hundred times over in Germany, Britain, France,
Russia, and Japan. In essence, World War II was locked armies,
scorched earth, executed prisoners, saturation bombings, atomic
attack, slave labor, gas ovens, the cream of a male generation
dead or brutalized, a barbaric contest of attrition ending only in
enemy collapse and unconditional surrender.

These disasters and the uneasy peace that followed spoke of
the human condition in those terrible years. It was one of spiritual
bankruptcy and debasement. Indeed, man had the potential to
destroy his world. But as it was, the overwhelming power of the
Allies prevailed over the helpless exhaustion of the Axis. The conquered took to their knees, and their abasement was called peace.
It was an old and tragic story, told rigorously and repetitiously
by history but apparently never learned.

Americans, I suspect, were least prepared to understand their
part in the international tribalism that became the fury of World
War II. No nation entered the war more unprepared or ended it
as invincible and unhurt. Our power—uneducated by suffering,
unchecked by defeat, unhampered by restraint—had slowly risen
to rage against the enemy. But it was not an unmixed blessing,
for it infected the men who wielded it, even as it won a victory
of sorts. And so, soldiers like us found no contradiction in seeking
peace while prowling morbidly among the cadavers of Münster,
"shacking up" in Paris, killing a helpless prisoner, dumping six
tons of white phosphorus on Dresden, or vaporizing Hiroshima.
Consequently, we "emissaries of peace," as our leaders called us,
had no human resources to quench the hell raging over Europe
and the Far East—except to crush it.

It was no excuse then or now, or even the slightest solution, to
justify ourselves by claiming that Nazis and Japs were barbarians
before we were or by saying that fire at white heat can only be

put out by fire. Barbarism is sufficiently subtle, diverse, and general to be a common liability, as an impartial reading of history suggests. And fire added to fire is liable to burn out of control or to smolder for another day and another blaze. As Pope Pius XII said, "The savagery of this war is but seed for the next conflict."

Nor did the public conduct of our leaders give any evidence that they appreciated the contribution of foreign policy to war. They could not admit, for example, the relationship between Nazism and a humiliated Germany following World War I and Versailles. They could not admit that American segregation of blacks influenced Hitler's "master race" Aryanism. They could not admit that the alleged "appeasement" of Munich—with us in high approval—was a crafty tactic intended to set the two giants of the Right and the Left, Hitler and Stalin, at one another's throats, there to exhaust themselves while the Western democracies rested secure. In other words, our leaders could or would do nothing to stop Hitler before he became unstoppable. And despite their hopes, it was too late to stop him when relations became nose-to-nose. It was too late for anything but patriotic righteousness and war.

The same held true in relationship with Japan. Our leaders could not admit that Japan learned its nationalist lessons too well from the West, particularly from America. Japan learned its industrialism from Europe and from us, its foreign policy from Our Open Door policy, its imperialism from our model empire in the Pacific, its antiwhite racism from our treatment of Orientals. As the showdown loomed, to admit that Japan was using our logic against us would be the worst imaginable blunder, even a form of treason. Japan, better mobilized for war than ourselves and more aware of the inevitability of conflict, knocked off the chip at Pearl Harbor, and we went to war.

The failure of our leadership went deeper still, at colossal expense to the American people. It is a fact that our people did not want war, nor—to give them credit—did our leaders. But they made no attempt to explain publicly that the Open Door was our foreign policy, that we were *not* isolationist, that we instigated international tension by the aggressiveness of global profit-seeking, and that only two choices remained—back up our economy or go to war. Who knows? The people, who pay for war with blood, labor, and treasure, might have chosen a readjustment of their economy and a lower standard of living to the horror of world war.

Nonetheless, alternatives to war were disallowed because, as our leaders knew, the Open Door policy allowed none. It implicated us too deeply in Western capitalism, now fighting for its life against Germany; it implied defense of American interests abroad; it grew from a value system as much public as it was official; and it viewed war as an ultimate sanction on the political process. A highly developed form of economic aggression, the Open Door policy needed willingness to go to war as the measure of its credibility.

Then as now, our leadership commanded sufficient support to preclude any choices offered to the American public which ignored the Open Door. Our leadership knew the temper of its constituency, the financial-industrial giants and, beneath them, the grass-roots capitalists. The sanction for war came from all of them and from their attitudes regarding profits, property, standards of living, racial separation, cultural superiority, and foreigners (tolerance if they were white, contempt if they were colored). For politicians to question attitudes like these would be to question the essence of American nationalism. Furthermore, it would be to question their very power base and their power itself.

American leadership also failed to grasp that its conduct of World War II augured disastrously for the future. If the history of World War I and its aftermath taught any lesson, it was that the unconditional surrender of Germany should never again be repeated. Nevertheless, the Allied aim was precisely that, both against Germany and Japan. The furious application of Allied power—total war—brought both nations down to crushing and abject defeat. Assumptions were held that the more total the defeat, the less prospect for national resurgence and future war. Assumptions were also held that even as power decided defeat, it also dictated justice. Nuremberg serves as an an oblique example of this: The Nazis *should* have been indicted for the mass murder of Jews and displaced persons, but who could indict the Americans and the British for Dresden and Hamburg, or the Americans for Hiroshima and Nagasaki? Since power defined justice, gas ovens became more unjust than fire storms or atomic vaporizing.

Nonetheless, events still tend to balance the scales, and the world now employs the principles of Nuremberg to indict our intervention in Vietnam.

> *The situation in the world today is not primarily the result of natural difficulties which follow a great war. It is chiefly due to the fact that one nation has not only refused to cooperate in the establishment of a just and honorable peace, but—even worse—has actually sought to prevent it.*—HARRY S TRUMAN, MARCH, 1948 [1]

Long before the war, pursuing its wretched course across Europe and the Far East, finally ground to a halt in 1945, it had already been condemned as "total war" and as morally reprehensible by Pope Pius XII. The combatants gave him scant attention; neither side troubled to deny that it was "total war" or to admit the slightest obligation to curb indiscriminate destruction and terrorism. Justification for their convenient deafness came from many sources, but especially from two: the new efficacy of propaganda as a weapon to insure nationalist—and collectivist—survival, plus the moral mandate given to both the Allied and the Axis powers from their national churches.

Neither side, therefore, had scruples about total war—after all, who was to stop them save themselves? The Allies initially made an outraged and plausible case against Axis aggression and atrocities. But as their own mobilization increased in power to equal that of the Axis, causing a mutual pattern of indiscriminate sav-

agery and attrition, strictly moral claims lost their plausibility.
Both sides determined to unleash whatever destructive power
they controlled in order to break enemy resistance and to win.
Policies like these required a final attack upon enemy resources
as total as the attack upon the war machine dependent on those
resources. Beyond the front-line forces—army, navy, air force, and
logistics—war potential became the object of attack: industry,
homes, the old, the young, even the unborn. Mutual agreement
forbid only poison gas—a mutually pragmatic course, to be sure.
Aside from that, destruction was limited only by the power and
will to employ it.

Max Born has commented significantly about the progressive
relaxation of restraint in the use of modern weapons, beginning
with the decision of the German General Staff to employ chemical
warfare in World War I.[2] With one moral defeat came another:
the collapse of the principle that civilians be immune from military attack. The German bombing of Rotterdam, Oslo, Coventry,
Bristol, Liverpool, and London prompted retaliation on Hamburg,
Dresden, Essen, Kassel, Munich, Cologne, and Berlin. Obviously,
saturation bombing weakened any remaining scruples, making
Hiroshima and Nagasaki more "logical" decisions. The two nuclear experiments on Japan caused hardly a tremor of conscience
in the Western world. The main reactions were rather ones of relief that against all expectations such crimes could end the war
and force the peace. There was little or no anxiety expressed over
the fact that these crimes made all previous criteria of inhumanity
obsolescent.

Max Born also illustrates the relationship between the application of modern weaponry and the increase in civilian deaths. The
moral defeat implicit in one causes the slaughter of the other.

In World War I, the total number of killed was approximately 10
million, 95% of whom were soldiers and 5% civilians. In World War II,
over 50 million were killed, comprising almost equal numbers of soldiers
and civilians (52% to 48%). During the war in Korea, of the nine million
dead, 84% were civilians and only 16% soldiers.[3]

Judging from dire statistics like these and from the burnt-earth

character of the Vietnam war, one can fairly assume that casualties there are 90 per cent civilian, or nine civilians dead for every
soldier.

There is no gain in trying to isolate responsibility for the colossal crimes of World War II and the cold war unless one is willing
to assume responsibility for oneself and one's country, in the hope
that doing so will check the fateful slide of humanity toward
larger and more devastating war. In a practical sense, Americans
express their responsibility to mankind by virtue of their country's
life and foreign policy. Indeed, national attitudes and values come
to universal culmination in foreign policy; it is here that national
values become a world view. And though responsibility may be
obscure and complicated, it is there, as frightening as it is challenging.

In view of this, both personal responsibility and historical fact
are jeopardized by contending that the primary guilt for the cold
war rests with Hitler and Nazi Germany. Most cold-war historians
assume that Hitler's mad attempt to unify Eastern and Central
Europe brought the United States and the Soviet Union into an
inevitable clash from the Baltic to the Black Sea. While acknowl-
edging that Hitler's ambition made a violent, if somewhat
remote, contribution to eventual cold war, Americans need to
remember that two other factors were more immediate and perhaps more critical: America's conduct of World War II and sec-
ondly, America's postwar diplomacy, which stemmed logically
and intransigently from the Open Door policy. The application
of the latter showed little awareness of twenty million Russian
war-dead, a Soviet economy verging on collapse, and aspirations
that had immeasurably more to do with rebuilding and security
than with aggressive expansion.

What of our conduct of the war? Without reviewing its early
history, we can say that the late stages of World War II featured
one overwhelming factor—American power. To begin with, our
industrial might was of such a magnitude and quality that it was
capable of waging a two-front war designed to bring powerful
and ruthless enemies to their knees. As early as November, 1943,

Donald Nelson, Roosevelt's head of the War Production Board, maintained that production of war material was so enormous that two years of war, vast allocations to our allies, and a double-front involvement could not consume it all.'

We applied this power to the enemy with growing vindictiveness, and finally with moral abandon. No period, no war, or no nation can match the unimaginable destruction with which we pummeled the Axis at the war's end: Dresden, Hamburg, Essen, Tokyo, Yokohama, Hiroshima, Nagasaki. These scenes of incomparable ruin qualified us as history's most violent nation, a distinction that we have never relinquished since. But American power did more than just crush Germany and Japan—it freed a whole flood of mysterious fears and hatreds in erstwhile friends and enemies alike. The Soviets, for example, knew us as uneasy friend and probable enemy. And we gave them little assurance that we would seek their friendship after the fall of Hitler—except on our own terms.

To give the Russians credit, they understood well that without American aid and ordnance they would not have been able to absorb the main thrust of the Nazi fury or avoid collapse. But their recollection of prewar relations with America was lively enough to tell them that an alliance quickly forged by Nazi fanaticism could as quickly evaporate. Finally, they suspected with good reason that Hiroshima and Nagasaki were trump cards against them—preliminaries to "negotiations from strength."

So much for American employment of power, which declined in wisdom even as it grew in strength. Very simply, our power in the war and in postwar diplomacy aimed to reassert the Open Door, which in turn was a gut need issuing directly from an organically overproductive capitalist system. The Russians understandably faced the imperatives of American expansionism with some apprehension. A few historical instances might help to support their suspicions.

They remembered painfully well American collaboration with British, French, Italians, Serbs, Rumanians, and Greeks in attempts to nullify the Russian Revolution, as well as the Allied naval blockade that effectively closed all Russian ports. They remembered how the United States shunned the League of Nations, whereas they themselves joined the League even after Germany and Japan had deserted it. Sumner Welles's appraisal of that situation is accurate: "When the Soviet Union entered the League, even the most obstinate were soon forced to admit that it was the only major power which seemed to take the League seriously." [5]

They remembered how Maksim Litvinov, their Commissar of Foreign Affairs, begged for League intervention when Hitler occupied and remilitarized the Rhineland, and how Britain voted against his resolution. They understood the British hope—shared and supported by us—of making an arch anti-Communist out of Hitler, of encouraging his ambitions to the East rather than to the West, so that Hitler and Stalin at one another's jugular might serve as an insurance policy for the West—in other words, the hope that "dominoes" in Eastern Europe might serve as canaries whetting Hitler's appetite, giving him the ambition to gulp as big a bird as Russia.

They also remembered how Stalin despaired of Western support against Hitler and was thus forced into virtual accommodation with him. Stalin had, it would seem, ample proof of Western deceit and hostility. He knew, or at least suspected, that the Chamberlain-Hitler "deal" at Munich partitioning Eastern Europe had him very much in mind as the victim, that British intelligence gave Russia a maximum life-span of six months before Hitler's armies, and that only time could prepare him for the inevitable onslaught from the West. Thus, the Hitler-Stalin pact was signed.

Insofar as he had to be right—that is, in regard to Russia—Stalin was right. Russia took the major fury of the Nazi blitzkrieg, thereby contributing precious time—perhaps even viability—to the Allies. Had the German thrust been solely toward the West, Russia would have had little reason to become embroiled, and all of Europe including Britain might have been engulfed.

Despite Russia's agony under German invasion, the Allies delayed initiating a western front year after year, for they were following Churchill's strategy that the future configuration of Europe

ought to dictate Allied plans. Instead, they opened the North
African campaign and invaded Sicily, pursuing victories with the
costly struggle up the Italian peninsula. All were of dubious military value. When the Allies invaded France in June, 1944, they
fulfilled promises delivered so late—some twenty-eight months
late—that they benefited the Russians hardly at all.[6]

All of this may serve as historical preface to other unpopular
and widely denied considerations. The Russia that faced the Allies in Eastern Europe at the war's end was a bear with very
nearly mortal wounds. No nation in history had suffered so griev-
ously from war. Twenty million dead lay at the rear of the Red
Army; the living remained starved and in shock; field and industry had suffered nearly total ruin. The only noteworthy political
asset that Stalin possessed was the superb Red Army, but its manpower was desperately needed for industrial and food production.
Conditions were hardly auspicious for bargaining, let alone expansion. Stalin, much more of a nationalist than an imperialist,
had to confront a staggering array of national problems as well
as hostile allies—above all, America, at that point in the full flush
of its superpower status. Not one to indulge himself with nervous
scruples over total war, Stalin could not have been other than
fearful about America's weaponry or its deadly—and oblique—
decision to experiment upon Japan with nuclear bombs.

As the record has it, the American stick against Russia was the
incineration of Hiroshima and Nagasaki. The carrots came slightly
later, but they were small, ambiguous, and grudgingly offered.
Russia appealed for reconstruction loans with no strings attached;
they were refused. America offered inclusion into the Marshall
Plan; it was refused. Refusal in both cases rose from antithetical
aims: American ambitions on the one hand to apply the Open
Door policy to Russia, and Russian insistence on the other to rebuild its economy and security without foreign interference. Russia rejected the Marshall Plan because to accept it would force allocations of Russian raw materials for Western Europe and would
allow the United States to interfere with Russian internal affairs
and even to have certain controls over foreign policy. Obviously,
Stalin could not agree to proposals like these. To agree would be

to invite Western interference—even control—in Soviet economics and politics, to compromise the objectives of Russian nationalism, and to replace the recently eliminated Nazi threat with a different Western one.

To claim this is not to whitewash Stalin or to give him a gratuitous reputation as a victim of Western ambition and greed. Neither is it to ignore his crimes: his purge and slaughter of opponents, his massacre of the kulaks, his sellout of the Spanish Loyalists, his hypocrisy toward the Chinese Revolution, the whole appalling catalog of ruthless opportunism which scored his leadership. But he was no Hitler, despite our efforts at comparison. What he did was for Mother Russia in light of its relationship to the West, its disastrous suffering during the war, its available and unavailable options after the peace. As for options, Stalin did not have many, but being the fervent nationalist that he was, he decided on a course aimed at guaranteeing Russia's autonomy, reconstruction reparations from Eastern Europe, rejection of the Marshall Plan, and a western military buffer guarding Russia's borders from any new threat, including resurgent German militarism.

The point at issue is that Russia did not create the cold war, as our angry and tiresome propaganda would have it. If our policy had been more wise and humane, Russia would have reacted differently, just as we would have probably followed the Russian course if our places had been switched. As it was, however, Russia reacted to Western—that is, American—power with human predictability, and out of that reaction came the cold war. We wanted the Open Door—economic and political entrance—in Europe and even in Russia. Russia wanted redevelopment loans without strings, German industrial machinery, and security against any repetition of the terrible German invasion. Out of their respective nationalisms, therefore, both sides held stubbornly to their aims, and the ominous impasse that resulted was the cold war. Nonetheless, Russia's exhaustion gave her few alternatives to the course she took, whereas we had many alternatives that we refused to take.

Alternatives we had, but our refusal to take them stemmed

mostly from the determinism implicit in the Open Door policy
and from our use of the atomic bomb to give the policy credibility. For purposes of clarity here, one might deal separately with
policy and policy's weapon. But it is critical to see that the Open
Door and the bomb excluded alternatives for us, just as internal
ruin excluded alternatives for Stalin.

The world view that preoccupied our leaders during and after
the war was one of American predominance. G. L. Arnold, an
Englishman generally favorable to our aims, said that the American world view then was based

upon the expectation of a prolonged era of peace, Anglo-American
hegemony (with the aid of China) in the United Nations and in the
world generally, free trade outside the Soviet orbit and gradual liberali-
zation within, a weakened and profoundly pacific Russia far behind the
Western powers in the utilization of atomic energy.[7]

A brief sketch may isolate evidence of such a view:

Item 1: In the winter of 1941–42 America declined to discuss
with Russia its desire to settle Eastern Europe's postwar boundaries as they were before Hitler's invasion.
The reason was Pearl Harbor and other military losses
—no strength for "negotiations from strength."

Item 2: Nearly three years later, in the fall of 1944, the same
issue reopened when the Russian counteroffensive
against Hitler began. Even the British wanted to negotiate Russia's "windows to the West," but Roosevelt
and Hull refused, standing by the philosophy of the
Open Door. As a consequence, Stalin must have concluded that he would "have to fight at the peace conference in order to get our western frontiers."[8]

Item 3: A tentative ten-billion-dollar reconstruction loan for
Russia, engineered by Donald M. Nelson and Eric
Johnston and eagerly desired by the Russians, who in
exchange promised in 1943 to enter the war against
Japan, was finally torpedoed by men like Averell Harri-
man, James Forrestal, Bernard Baruch, and George
Kennan, staunch anti-Communists all.

Item 4: At Yalta Stalin bargained unsuccessfully with American
power on all but one issue—economic rights in Man-

churia in exchange for American predominance in China. On other questions—Poland, Russian presence in the northern Iranian oil fields, Russian security in the Black Sea region—he made severe compromises, mostly in the hope of gaining agreement in other areas.

Item 5: Russian intellectuals like Varga and Aleksandrov published highly favorable views of Western capitalism in 1946 and 1947, dwelling upon its ability to stabilize itself in the postwar era. *Izvestia* itself had taken the same tack in early 1945, consistently praising the vigor of the American economy. Russia as a whole was answered by Churchill's Iron Curtain speech of 1946 and by the Truman Doctrine in 1947.

Item 6: President Truman led the ideological fight against Russia by reviving the comparison between Nazi Germany and Stalinist Russia. He justified American inflexibility not by giving its reason, the Open Door strategy, but by reference to the "appeasement" that Munich produced—appeasement that America would refuse to repeat. Among other examples of firmness, America terminated lend-lease to Russia after Japan's defeat. As for the Truman Doctrine, Henry Stimson and Henry Wallace admitted that it was very nearly an act of war.[9]

It now appears almost certain that American leaders knew enough about Russia's internal weakness to realize that it had neither the desire nor the resources to expand like Hitler's Germany or to consider seriously another war. Our decision to checkmate Russia came rather from the dynamics of the Open Door, from the fear of a postwar depression, and from a craving for what Henry R. Luce called "an American Century" in which, as a leading oil-industry leader asserted, America would be "the majority stockholder in this corporation known as the world." [10] In fact, the American leaders' knowledge of the basic realities and dangers of the Open Door policy went much deeper than they were usually willing to admit. In 1943 William L. Clayton, who had headed one of the world's largest export cotton firms and who joined the Roosevelt Administration during the war, said this:

The international economic policies of nations have more to do with creating conditions which lead to war than any other single factor. . . . As a matter of fact, if we want to be honest with ourselves, we will find that many of the view that are freely utilize other countries for producing have their counterpart in the United States.[11]

In light of such realities, our use of the atomic bomb against Japan follows a logic only lately come to light. The American leadership conceived, tested, and employed the bomb as a master card in cold war strategy—as the gun behind the Open Door.

It must be remembered that the Russians, in response to Allied pressure, promised to attack Japan three months after an armistice in Europe. With mounting Allied successes in the Far East, however it was decided at Potsdam in July, 1945, to keep Russia out of the war with Japan. President Truman, General George Marshall, and Secretary of War Henry Stimson agreed on this, and their agreement necessarily implied using the atomic bomb as quickly as possible. In their view, the *coup de grâce* against Japan had to be massive, new, employed with maximum surprise.

Marshall, for one, had changed his mind about using the bomb. Some time before Potsdam, he believed that "the impact of Russion entry on the already hopeless Japanese may well be the decisive action levering them into capitulation." [12] Apparently, however, the sudden success with which the Manhattan Project made the atomic bomb available led him to conclude—like Truman and Stimson—that the bomb would be gainfully employed against Japan if it stopped Russia in Asia and warned her in Eastern Europe.

Truman excused the bomb's use by an explanation tailored specifically for the American public: "The dropping of the bomb stopped the war, and saved millions of lives." [13] He meant, of course, American lives; or he meant that staggering numbers of Japanese atomic casualties would break any resistance and remove the need for invasion and the bloody losses that would entail.

Military men, however, and Allied leaders other than the Ameri-

cans opposed using nuclear weapons. General Eisenhower told
Secretary Stimson in 1945: "I am against it on two counts. First,
the Japanese are ready to surrender and it isn't necessary to hit
them with that awful thing. Second, I hate to see our country be
the first to use such a weapon." [14] His opinion reflected precisely
that of the Joint Chiefs of Staff, who, excepting Marshall, ad-
vised that Japan would probably surrender unconditionally without nuclear bombing or an invasion. Admiral William Leahy took
the same view after the bombing as before it: "It is my opinion
that the use of this barbarous weapon at Hiroshima and Nagasaki was of no material assistance in our war against Japan. The
Japanese were already defeated and ready to surrender." [15] Admiral
Ernest King judged the bomb unnecessary. Even General Curtis
LeMay, never notorious for queasiness about total air attack upon
cities and civilians, joined with General Henry Arnold in the
official Air Force position by stating: "Whether or not the
atomic bomb should be dropped was not for the Air Force to de-
cide, but explosion of the bomb was not necessary to win the war
or make an invasion unnecessary." [16]

Similar opinions came from Britain before Hiroshima. General
Hastings Ismay believed that the Japanese were "tottering," and
like Eisenhower and Leahy, he viewed the suggestion of atomic
bombing with "revulsion." Churchill himself, feeling that Russia's entry into the war against Japan was conducive to surrender,
wrote this: "It would be a mistake to suppose that the fate of Japan
was settled by the atomic bomb. Her defeat was certain before
the first bomb fell." [17]

Furthermore, military appraisals ventured before the bombing
received substantial backing from a series of postsurrender studies.
The best of these was the United States Strategic Bombing Survey. Its conclusion was forceful and unequivocal: "Japan would
have surrendered even if the atomic bombs had not been dropped,
even if Russia had not entered the war, and even if no invasion
had been planned or contemplated."

If, then, the Japanese saw the end as soon as we, and if they
made feverish attempts to capitulate under the guarantees offered

the Emperor by President Truman, why was the atomic bomb used? (Then as now, exploration of the real reason is irrelevant to public support or opposition. Most Americans accepted, if not supported, Truman's justification without question. Indeed, the relief and joy which rose like a sigh from the nation following the bombing suggests that Americans were morally unequipped to judge any use of the bomb against any enemy if a brutal war would end thereby, at a substantial saving of American lives.)

In any event, America dropped the atomic bomb on Japan in order to intimidate Russia. That is to say, we wanted Japan knocked quickly out of the war so that the Soviets would have no reason to attack in the Far East and no reason to establish their power there. And at the same time, we wanted to give them good reason to tread cautiously in Europe. We dropped the bomb *against* the Russians but *on* the Japanese; both the bomb and its victims at Hiroshima and Nagasaki lent credibility to our determination to concede nothing to the Russians. Vannevar Bush, an important aide to Secretary Stimson, made that fact clear: Not only did the atomic bomb mean a quick end to the war with the Japanese but "it was delivered on time so that there was *no necessity* for *any concessions* [my italics] to Russia at the end of the war." [18] And J. Robert Oppenheimer, testifying on this point some years later, said, "Much of the discussion [of the bomb] revolved around the question raised by Secretary Stimson as to whether there was any hope at all of using this development to get less barbarous relations with the Russians." [19]

This presents another question: If the Russians needed to be convinced of American power, why not convince them with a peaceful and highly publicized explosion of the bomb, *without* sacrificing Hiroshima and Nagasaki? The answer would appear to be that the bomb had been developed as an ultimate diplomatic tool, and once available on this basis, it controlled the thinking of those responsible for its being. Secretary Stimson, who helped formulate the decision to attack Japan with atomic weapons, later regretted the bomb's influence on the hard line taken with Russia. But then it was too late for Stimson to do other than to suspect—and to admit somewhat—his tragic error.

Ironically enough, then, the responsibility for experimenting on human flesh with nuclear weaponry fell upon civilians—a fact at some variance with the nuclear aggressiveness so common among Pentagon militarists today. The President and men of Cabinet rank grilled several hundred thousand people on a nuclear spit while the best military minds in the Allied camp expressed virtual opposition.

Accordingly, it seems quite clear that the civilian decision to make an atomic laboratory of two great Asian cities stemmed from our resolve to force open the economic doors of the world. To accomplish this, we thought it necessary to intimidate the Russians with our power and with our willingness to use it. As an atomic scientist said following an interview with Secretary of State James Byrnes in May, 1945: "Mr. Byrnes did not argue that it was necessary to use the bomb against the cities of Japan in order to win the war. . . . Mr. Byrnes' view was that our possessing and demonstrating the bomb would make Russia more manageable in Europe." [20]

The most destructive and bloody war in history finally ended, but only at a cost of proportionate brutalization to mankind. And then the cold war began—brutally, stupidly, ominously, perhaps irrevocably. Obviously, it had two conflicting parties at the outset, and to that extent the culpability remains dual. Nonetheless, the expansionist nature of the American economy is not debatable, and its thrust was determinist enough to subject Russia, its major global opponent, to its threats. Russia reacted—perhaps had to react—to maintain its national sovereignty; a familiar push-and-shove situation emerged, and the cold war was born.

A greater fear to American leaders at the war's close than fear of the Russians or another major war was the "bust" side of the economic "boom-bust" cycle. President Truman believed—with a powerful consensus from business leaders—that war prosperity would lapse into a depression as serious as that of the 1930's unless our economy found markets and similar safety valves to replace war production. Truman knew that America could not re-

vert to our prewar industrial status; the productive capacity that
won the war was still in existence, and it could not be dismantled
without essential changes in free-enterprise capitalism. Furthermore, the economy's potency was such that it would satisfy consumer demand from an appliance starved public in astoundingly
short order. Since a switch from capitalism—in other words, a shift
in power—was unthinkable, our leaders could not allow the economy to paint itself into a corner by outproducing its domestic
market. Its historic frontier must rather be enlarged—a point
about which our leaders refused to debate, a point about which
the world was not allowed to debate.

We went back to the Open Door policy as if it were a love
affair rudely interrupted by the war. Russia stood as the only
major roadblock to our worldwide economic hegemony; all other
nations either accepted our ambitions or were helpless to withstand them. And by a quality of reasoning which may be one of
the outstanding limitations of power, our leaders determined to
secure domestic peace (prosperity) at the price of world unrest.
They must have known—or suspected in their better moments—
that the world would never accept American imperialist advantage. Nevertheless, they decided that foreigners *must* accept it,
and that American military power would provide the clinching
argument.

Not only does all contemporary evidence suggest their preference for this course but so also does the central theme of our
history, which springs directly from the assumption that we must
expand into an empire in order to exist as a nation. The risks of
nuclear war were therefore to be chosen before the risks of
domestic friction or uprising. Our leaders feared a desperate and
impoverished world less than they feared the American public. A
total overhaul of our economics or variations in the free-enterprise system were never considered as alternatives. Who in power
chooses to put himself out of power—or out of business?

Therefore, in the sense that the Open Door became the total
rationale behind our domestic and foreign policy and behind the
whole structural purpose and mechanism of American society,

there could be no tampering with it. Foreign profits had long been understood as the difference between domestic prosperity and depression, between domestic peace and possible revolution. Consequently, foreign profits became a necessity for the survival of capitalistic democracy. This was reason enough for an unswerving course in their favor. This was also reason enough for the Open Door policy to become the diplomatic hopper grinding forth every major policy decision, from the Office of Economic Opportunity to intervention in Vietnam.

If such claims seem broad, evidence exists that the Open Door policy not only provoked the cold war but did so by controlling all aspects of our foreign policy, from nuclear diplomacy to foreign aid. A case in point was the Acheson-Lilienthal-Baruch plan for the atom, in which the United States, with apparent fairness and concern, proposed international control of the atom. But in doing so, the plan neither promised that we would discontinue manufacturing the atomic bomb, nor did it set any precise time for our releasing the bomb to an international agency. We expected the Russians to respond by trusting us with monopoly of nuclear weapons for an indefinite period and by granting an international authority virtual control over their nuclear economic affairs, which is diplomatic language for *all* economic affairs. What was really attempted by us under the plan was quite analogous to Secretary of State Philander Knox's proposal to internationalize the Manchurian railways in 1909, or to President Truman's attempt to do the same with the Danubian waterways in 1945. Internationalization meant Americanization, or at the least, a facade of multination control under which American interests could get their way. J. Robert Oppenheimer, a member of the Acheson-Lilienthal committee, admitted candidly: "The prevalent view saw in the problems of atomic energy . . . an opportunity to cause a decisive change in the whole trend of Soviet policy." [21]

In a reversal of roles, America would have indignantly refused. As it was, Russia did exactly that. Bernard Baruch explained why with substantially the same reason the Russians gave: "[Russia] has no intention of permitting a situation whereby the national

economy of the Soviet Union or particular branches of that economy would be placed under foreign control." [22] Secretary of Commerce Henry Wallace, on the other hand, put the issue in terms
of reciprocal justice:

We should be prepared to judge [Russia's] requirements against the
background of what we ourselves and the British have insisted upon as
essential to our respective security. We should be prepared, even at the
expense of risking epithets of appeasement, to agree to reasonable
Russian guarantees of security.[23]

But hardly anyone in power agreed with Wallace, whose de-
viant views led to his elimination from Truman's Cabinet on
September 20, 1946. Without doubt, the Russians judged accurately the reasons for his firing, just as they judged accurately
the cancellation of an Export-Import Bank loan to Czechoslovakia
in October. They retaliated by naming Andrei Zhdanov as their
chief propagandist, and his vulgar anti-Americanism competed
favorably with the anti-Soviet diatribes of Truman and Churchill.
The Russians had supposedly learned another lesson from us: the
cold-war value of ideological propaganda. Nonetheless, Zhdanov began his new assignment only after the Varga debates of
May, 1947—in which American capitalism was praised—had ended.
    George Kennan's policy of containment gives another example
of the psychological hold the Open Door had on American policy-
makers. A moralist-diplomat somewhat more broad and subtle
than John Foster Dulles but with the same Puritan fervor, Kennan believed that external containment could force internal liberation, depending on the power and determination of the container
and on the pent-up resentments of the contained. It was on the
second count that he miscalculated, for he obviously knew little of
the Russian rank and file's views of leadership, oppression, American liberation. That Russians might have preferred *their* leadership—because it was *theirs*, despite its oppression—to American interference was incomprehensible to him.
    And so he could remark that the Soviets were moving "inexor-
ably along the prescribed path, like a persistent toy automobile
wound up and headed in a given direction, stopping only when it

meets with some unanswerable force" [24]—an analysis more aptly applied to his own country. He failed to understand that containment was far more a military measure than a political one, or that given the postwar world, a successful Open Door policy demanded more of the military and less of the political. It may have been evasion or blunder, but it still left him free to deplore American "overmilitarization" a decade later. And though he would admit in 1957 that containment had not prevented Russian internal development, it was not the same as admitting that containment united and mobilized the Russian people as had no other single factor.

The Truman Doctrine of 1947 formally sanctioned Kennan's view. From that time on, the United States wanted a serious political—or military—offensive against the Communists. We ignored negotiations with the Russians and evaded the framework of the United Nations. The offensive reflected the hopes of President Truman, Dean Acheson, and Averell Harriman that Russia would be intimidated and would allow access to its own orbit. But if the Truman Doctrine failed in this objective, it succeeded in another —the cold war. Both alternatives, Russian submission or the cold war, fitted our domestic needs and the Open Door policy.

Our leaders minted the Marshall Plan in the same coin. Undeniably, it expressed a generous humanitarian purpose. The war had left Western Europe prostrate and quite incapable of regaining its economic feet without massive outside aid. Nevertheless, the pride that Americans take in the Marshall Plan must be qualified by several national-interest factors. Domestic depression loomed— Marshall himself explained his proposal to Congress in "business terms" (and upon business depended the survival of "democracy" at home). Furthermore, other allies—Chinese and Latin Americans—expressed an equal desperation of need. But other allies did not promise, as did Western Europe, stable returns upon American loans and investments. Other allies did not possess, as did Western Germany, France, and the Low Countries, industrial infrastructures temporarily ruined but capable of being restored easily enough to give promise of becoming economic outposts of the American empire.

With the Marshall Plan began a progressive trend in the Open Door policy: international credit to buy American surpluses. Later on, with Europe invigorated and booming, the Agency for International Development took on the same task in the Third World. Both provisions unwittingly express the fact that the guts of corporate capitalism is credit—credit at home and credit abroad. Foreign credit is substantially the tale of some 120 billion dollars of foreign "aid" given by America to the world since 1945.

Not surprisingly, the Russians greeted the invitation to participate in the Marshall Plan with a suspicion grounded in intimate experience with our Open Door diplomacy. As they saw it, the Marshall Plan threatened Eastern European economies and, indeed, their own. With even greater alarm, the Russians saw in it the probability of a rearmed Germany, a probability that reawakened in them nasty recollections of life under Hitler, but this time under the flag of the American superpower. Baruch's plan to monopolize atomic energy under international control, Kennan's plan to contain Russia's borders, Marshall's plan to monopolize Eurasian economics—this is how the Russians viewed the guileless altruism of America's diplomatic package.

Again, what were Stalin's options? His official line and policy hardened into measures of brutal expediency, but mainly in Eastern Europe only. Serious concessions elsewhere had already been made to American pressure: in Greece, where Stalin allowed the British and Americans to cool the Greek Revolution; in Iran, whose oil fields were under American control; at both ends of the Black Sea, which were mostly abandoned to American power. But in Eastern Europe Russia stood pat on the issue of nationalist integrity and survival. William Appleman Williams sketches the main lines of the Russians' forced consolidation there:

They initiated a program of general political repression in Rumania. They sharply curtailed freedom of the press in Bulgaria, Rumania, and eastern Germany. They shot the Peasant Party leader Patlov in Bulgaria. And within the year the Communist Party in Czechoslovakia seized a monopoly of political power.[25]

Action and reaction, one might call this—or the dynamics of

great-power rivalry. The most astonishing aspect of our policy is that our leaders assumed it would have no reaction, or that reaction could be channeled by American power into eventual American benefit. Meanwhile, cold-war policy took a frightful toll at home. Truman's unbalanced condemnation of Russia as the sole responsible party for the cold war, enthusiastically abetted by the militarist caste, helped to open the McCarthy era, enkindling in the process unsuspected reservoirs of paranoia and self-righteousness in the American people. Reinhold Niebuhr became America's cold-war theologian. His influence on the moralistically minded men of the State Department was such that George Kennan could call him "the father of us all."

If Russia was contained but not liberated, it is true to say that Western Europe was also contained—assimilated—within America's "free world" scheme but not liberated. In the lexicon of the Open Door policy, "liberation" means development under American economic and political tutelage while operating under the myth of self-determination. But repression works on both sides of the line of containment, and though the style we impose on Western Europe is profitable, that does not make it liberating.

The Chinese Revolution of 1949 offered another opportunity to apply containment policy. Here again, our intent was to promote counterrevolution within the People's Republic and to restore Chiang Kai-shek or someone as well disposed to our predominance. Measures similar to those employed against Russia were launched: propaganda drives, military harassment, trade restrictions and collective pacts, organized opposition in the United Nations. Critics have called this policy transplant "unimaginative," "rigid," and "provocative"—sophomoric observations that fail to consider the link between expansionist economics and expansionist diplomacy. If one accepts the first—most critics do—one must accept the second. And most critics don't. Apparently they think that doing half the world's business is such a clean and upright enterprise that a rational foreign policy is inevitable. Such naïveté borders on irresponsibility. How can bureaucratic power permit its foreign policy to contradict its economics?

In any event, the Open Door policy, whether against Russia or China, Latin America or the Middle East, is the diplomatic definition of free enterprise corporatism, whose future hangs upon global mass consumerism under American patronage. We can be grateful that humanity, including growing segments of the American people, are beginning to say something significant about this economic policy. For it underlies our racism, it inspires war, and it is the other side of domestic and world poverty. None of these conditions alone is a threat to the world's peace. The American empire is, however, and the problems it gives rise to must be solved.

There are no prototypes of revolution in an affluent society. And yet the United States is in revolution—a revolution of its own creation. Both the revolutions we create abroad and the means we take to counter them are faithfully repeated at home. Our obsession with stability has taken a hideously ironic turn to make us enemies of the same ideas and the same quality of people that gave us self-determination. Now a world in revolution uses them against us.

The reason why we are antirevolutionary is simple; indeed, it is the same simple reason why we cannot accept it. The reason is our affluence, which like involuntary poverty, makes no provision for escape. Confront the affluent with freedom, and they will prefer their goods. In their own way, the affluent are as typically slavish as the poor, but their lot is all the more tragic because it is voluntary. Their usual freedom of choice is to insulate themselves against change, to reject the revolution of values and institutions that alone could save them.

Robert Kennedy now lies with his brother John, Medgar Evers, and Martin Luther King. Meanwhile, the nation compulsively condemns its own violence and fumbles for a panacea: a commission on violence, a crime-control bill, new riot cars built by Cadillac. The solution is not so simple, one is tempted to warn; let's talk instead about the roots of violence in our society and about some of its fruit. Let's talk about the way America has institutionalized one of the most antisocial aspects of human nature, avarice. Let's talk about the lengths to which acquisitiveness will take us: starving children in Mississippi, South African investments, the CIA. Let's talk about profit-seeking being *the* catalyst of national life, for which we expend incredible effort and for which we risk life, limb, integrity, and salvation itself. Let's talk about roots of violence like these and then talk about their fruit: a capitalist economy and society, a class-conscious, racist, warfare, and exploitative state.

It is a curious fact that talk of violence always breaks down somewhere short of talk about injustice. Or perhaps it is not so curious, since the analysts of violence are invariably those most guilty of injustice or those most responsible for only talking about it. But there is a deeper reason for the omission: The analysts wish to preserve their power intact, all the while decrying violence and ignoring injustice.

This is a self-defeating policy, one might conclude, and an arrogant, presumptuous one. Let us not be too sure. The issue of whether power can maintain itself under its present assumptions is an enormously cloudy one. The first moves of an infant revolution now probe the establishment: draft refusal, ghetto anger, campus unrest, religious dissent, liberal disaffection. Yet the response of power has so far been more than equal to the probe. True enough, power has its vulnerabilities—Vietnamese heroism has exploded the myth of its invincibility, perhaps for all time. But the two faces of revolution against American power, foreign and native, are so absurdly unbalanced that they defy comparison. The Vietnamese struggle for survival and autonomy has changed from a movement to a revolution, whereas the American resistance has as yet no clear idea of identity, no threat to survival, no firm claim upon integrity. It is part-time, desultory, amateurish, and nearly as afraid of itself as the establishment is afraid of it. Aside from its rhetoric, it parts company with power only on minor issues, if its accomplishments are any criteria.

Yet the resistance view of itself is but one decisive factor leading to revolution or to something else—reform, for example. Of much more critical nature are other factors, and they lead more directly to revolution: capitalistic technocracy, concentrated wealth and power, infectious political representation, endemic racism, economic expansionism, militarism all of which fashion parliamentary politics into a forum for vested interests, freeze them against minority demands, and render them rigidly resistant to reform in any serious way.

To this formidable congeries of influence and force, the old axiom of violence can be applied. If the political, economic, and military communities breed enough violence to keep our country habitually on the brink of war and to make our domestic life humanly unliveable, and if reform is an alternative impossible to attain, what is left? Obviously, only a reaction by Americans to reassert their belief in human rights and political representation and to be something they are not now—moral and democratic men.

Beyond these generalities, the corollaries of action become painful and mysterious. Nonetheless, whatever their direction, they must assess the elements of control implicit in technology; they must assess whether capitalism is any longer viable as an economic theory, how political representation can be obtained, and how principles of self-determination can be a controlling force in foreign economics and policy. To these ends, power must be taken— it is rarely given; property and wealth must be redistributed as national, and then as world, assets; racism must be eliminated as our most costly liability; and militarism must be broken as a nearly autonomous power in economics and politics. This is not only the stuff of revolution, it *is* revolution. But as a reaction against institutionalized violence, it must be incomparably more intelligent, human, and just than the *status quo*. Otherwise, it will play the same essential game of violence, and good and bad alike will be swept away before the whirlwind.

Even more predictable in the process of revolution than human reaction to external violence is the revolutionary nature of human life. Indeed, if one neglects this truth or is dissuaded from it by the institutionalized conformity of technological society, he does it at expense to himself. Let it therefore be said, and said often: To be either human or Christian or both, man *must* be a revolutionary. To become himself, he must always be in revolt, constantly leaving his old man, confronting his personal smugness, injustice, and egotism, and challenging the corruption of public life and institutions. In this sense, is not revolution the personal and social expression of conversion? And does conversion ever cease to be a Christian duty and an unfinished business?

The Gospel teaches revolution mostly through the Lord's doctrine of His Cross and through His new commandment of love. Within the context of justice and love, the Lord taught His Cross as a necessary element in the struggle for humanity, with freedom and wisdom flowing from its acceptance and human retardation from its rejection. "Let him deny himself and take up his cross daily and follow me" (Luke 9:23). "He that will lose his life for my sake and the gospel, will save it" (Mark 8:35). "A new commandment I give you, that you love one another as I have loved you" (John 13:34). This is revolutionary talk and a revolutionary mandate coming directly from the Author and Lord of life. But it must be taken seriously.

Love makes revolutionaries of people because it engages both personal and public injustice at the same time. It is the great anticipator of interpersonal masochism, the great purifier of human relationships and institutions. And love's great expression is justice—justice never fully paid, never fully satisfying, never fully perfect.

The rights of revolution flow from the right to life. When people encounter unjust conditions of life which are involuntary, conditions that abuse their dignity or make their lives humanly impossible, they then have a right to rebel and make a revolution. That this right is taken should not be cause for astonishment, save on the part of those who oppress or know nothing of oppression. Nor is it a right taken often or irresponsibly, for survival must be weighed against the price of survival, and failure might mean death. People move into revolution not because of any specific deprivation, but because the most harrowing uncertainties become

preferable to known injustice. There comes a point where capitulation to tyranny becomes more intolerable than abhorrence for
revolution, where inaction is a worse injustice than that endured,
where hopelessness is a greater threat than risk, jail, or a bullet.

In time, the second American revolution will produce literature
worthy of it. And it will compare with that of the Founding
Fathers in principle, analysis, and outrage. The first of it has
already come out of our ghettos; student and establishment intellectuals will author more of it. As it matures under the pressure
of events, it will be written with less rage and more reasoned passion, perhaps with the quality of Thoreau, whose essay "Civil
Disobedience" is as valuable as it is neglected. Or it will be like a
relatively unknown speech of Lincoln in 1848, wherein he attacked
the Mexican War and President James Polk while giving his ideas
on revolution:

> Any people anywhere, being inclined and having the power, have the
> right to rise up, and shake off the existing government, and form a new
> one that suits them better. This is a most valuable—a most sacred right
> —a right, which we hope and believe, is to liberate the world. Nor is
> this right confined to cases in which the whole people of an existing
> government, may choose to exercise it. Any portion of such people that
> can, may revolutionize, and make their own, of so much of the territory
> as they inhabit. More than this, a majority of any portion of such people
> may revolutionize, putting down a minority, intermingled with, or
> near about them, who may oppose their movement. Such minority was
> precisely the case of the Tories of our own revolution. It is a quality of
> revolutions not to go by old lines, or old laws; but to break up both,
> and make new ones.[26]

Following the April, 1968, Baltimore uprisings that had their
immediately cause in Dr. Martin Luther King's murder, a young
professor at a local college had this exchange with one of his
students:

STUDENT: You're one of those flaming liberals who's always defending
           the niggers. What'll you say now after all the burning and
           looting in Baltimore? Far as I can see it, niggers are just
           thieves, and while they burn and loot, cops and troopers

stand and watch them. Niggers is just thieves, and we let
'em be that way.

PROFESSOR: They say that guilt and anger are often tied together. Is
that why you're so angry?

STUDENT: I'm not guilty about anything. This is what you usually do.
I ask you about niggers tearing up Baltimore, and you tell
me about guilt. I'll ask it again. What do you have to say
about niggers breakin' in and lootin' in Baltimore?

PROFESSOR: Well, maybe we can look at it this way. We're a nation of
thieves, and black people are finally getting into the act.
We stole this country from the people who lived here. We
built our wealth on the backs of slaves and, later on, immigrants from Asia and Europe. We stay rich by what we
take out of the Third World, a lot of it robbed. We've got
power, and when you've got power, you can steal what you
want and call it freedom. Black people are learning fast,
but they'll never be as good thieves as whites because we
won't let them.

The young professor's explanation deserves reflection. The
President's Riot Commission Report candidly admits that we have
institutionalized racism. Our war budget reminds us annually that
we have institutionalized war-making. A racist and war-making
society is not possible without institutionalized thievery—thievery
from the poor, from blacks, from man, from ourselves. Certainly
there is guilt, but we will not face it. We would rather flee to a
familiar escape of the rich and plead for law and order—instead
of law and justice.

The evidence at hand tells those who would listen that this
society cannot stand in its present, violent form. It needs revolution, not to destroy it—its most fearsome capability is self-destruc-
tion—but to save it, or to save whatever is worth saving. It has
caused revolution everywhere. Scores of Vietnams and ghettos rise
up to meet its violence, and such incidents are hopeful insofar as
they prove that man has not given up on himself. Were it not for
the various reactions of hope which spring up at every hand to
confront the imperial violence of our nation—reactions that gather
or crest into crisis—were it not for student uprisings, ghetto out-

rage, anti-American insurgency in every corner of the globe, fiscal emergencies that come from a world-police role, we would never learn what it means to be a Christian and a democratic man. We would never learn, in fact, that even in a technocracy the last and most priceless resource is man and his will to be human. As Lyndon Johnson has said, with the same uncomprehension as Caiaphas before Christ's murder, "We are learning today that being a human being is much more than we counted on!"

VI

Reflections on Church-State Covenants

≋≋≋

On Friday, October 27, 1967, we are entering the Customs House in Baltimore, Maryland, to deface the draft records there with our blood.

We shed our blood willingly and gratefully in what we hope is a sacrificial and constructive act. We pour it upon these files to illustrate that with them and in these offices begins the pitiful waste of American and Vietnamese blood 10,000 miles away. That bloodshed is never rational and seldom voluntary—in a word, it is nonconstructive. It does not protect life, but rather endangers it.

We wish neither notoriety nor labels of martyrdom or messianism. We desire merely to stand for human life and a human future. We realize painfully yet clearly that what we intend goes beyond the scope of Constitutional right and civil liberty and is therefore not to be taken lightly.

WAR AND PROPERTY: *We believe that war proves nothing except man's refusal to be man and to live with men. We say that man must end war, or war will end man. We deplore our country's hot and cold warring and its crime against the often unwilling and powerless bodies behind these files.*

145

Thus we unite with our servicemen against their real enemies. We shed our blood as they do theirs. We disrupt our lives as the draft does theirs.

We quarrel with the idolatry of property and with the war machine that makes property of men. We confront those countrymen to whom property means more than human life. We assert that property is often an instrument of massive injustice—like these files. Thus we feel that our discriminate destruction of this property is warranted in the interest of human life.

Nonetheless, we take every measure to protect the personnel here from hysteria or injury. We are content to remind them of their complicity in the untimely death of young soldiers, in the murder of innocent civilians, in the pain of parents, wives, and sweethearts. We ask their resignations.

AMERICA: *We agree that the United States is the greatest manufacturer and salesman of violence in the world today. We feel this is so because power rests not with the people to whom it belongs but with an economic, political, and military cabal whose aims can tolerate neither foreign autonomy nor domestic freedom.*

We charge that America would rather protect its empire of overseas profits than welcome its black people, rebuild its slums, and clean its air and water. Thus we have singled out inner-city draft boards for special attention.

We love our country and celebrate its greatness. But our love cannot accept its evil with silence and passivity. We withstand that evil with our consciences and our bodies and invite the punishment that this entails.

LAW: *We state that any law which forces men to kill and to face death furthers war as surely as it encourages men to profit from war. We assert that Vietnam is a rich man's war and a poor man's fight. It is an unjust war backed by unjust laws of conscription, tax benefits, and suppression of dissent.*

We indict such law with our consciences and our acts. We appeal to Americans to purge their law, to conform it to divine and humane law, to apply it impartially, and to build at home and abroad with it. We reject law when it protects injustice, since it is then not law but a travesty of it.

*Law is therefore under judgment with the evil it shields.
In light of this, we spurn any counsel that would bargain
for our benefit within the law, and stand on our merits
alone.*

*We seek neither to avoid detection nor to plan escape,
but submit to apprehension and the consequences of our
action.*

*We implore our countrymen to judge our stand against
this nation's Judeo-Christian tradition and against the horror in Vietnam and the impending threat of nuclear destruction—against, finally, the universal longing for justice
and peace.*

*We invite friends in the peace and freedom movements
to continue moving with us from dissent to resistance.*

*We ask God to be merciful and patient with us and
with all men. We hope that He will use our witness for his
blessed designs.*

> *Seriously yours,*
> REV. PHILIP BERRIGAN
> DAVID EBERHARDT
> THOMAS LEWIS
> REV. JAMES MENGEL

WHAT TO CALL THE ABOVE, VOW OR MANIFESTO?
No matter—it had no meaning until we did what we had to do. All
of us agreed emphatically that there are worse things to live with
than the Johnson Administration, our intervention in Vietnam, or
a few years in jail. And I don't mean the choice between Richard
Nixon and Hubert Humphrey as the next President of the United
States. I mean one's impotence and cowardice, one's complicity in
unimaginable, insane injustice. Make no mistake; America's guilt
is very broad and goes very deep, leaving no one untouched—least
of all, us.

The prospect of our "thing" was harrowing, but doing it was
ridiculously easy. The security guard, who had been ordered to
arm himself just prior to October 21 (the National Mobilization
in Washington), was providentially wandering about the building. We jockeyed a bit with receptionists to validate our presence,

and then strode into that obscene gallery where human lives were
reduced to a neat economy of print and code, where forms and
files held barely shaven boys in abeyance until the Department
of Defense (it has called itself the largest educational complex
in the world) schooled them in the bloody business of killing.

Trim secretaries looked up as we walked into their game preserve; they were as antiseptic and anonymous as the cabinets they
tended. Quite unconscious, they presided in detachment over the
tools of death like hens scratching away over a minefield. Yet here
the tools represented bodies. Men for all their culture, sophistication, and technology had not yet found a way to honor war without bodies, preferably those of eighteen- and nineteen-year-olds.
Many of the bodies filed were blacks whose value had soared in
wartime. Their housing would symbolically improve here in these
steel cabinets as they qualified for manhood in a white man's war.
Later, it would really improve in service barracks, although their
families would continue to languish in Baltimore's rotting slums.
Who said that war is hostile to progress?

We acted quickly and with relish. The blood we carried was
the biblical symbol of life. We would exorcise these files by pour-
ing our life upon them. We yanked open drawers, sloshed blood
upon their contents, moved on and repeated the act. The secretaries fooled us—we had anticipated screams and panic—by reacting with a certain animal courage, protesting first, then trying to
deter us. We spoke to them as kindly as we could, attempting
to give them statements and New Testaments. They would have
none of them; statements were ripped, New Testaments thrown
to the floor, and one particularly righteous woman bounced the
Scripture off Dave Eberhardt's head. It became apparent that certain basic energies had been freed and were now out of our control. Reflexes followed like those of Pavlov's dog, but enormously
more expressive.

A crowd gathered, but the police were slow in coming, the
FBI slower still. When the first nervous policeman came on the
scene, Dave Eberhardt befuddled him by saying, "As a taxpayer,
I want to protest the lax security around this place!"

The delay gave us time for more than humor. I reflected as we sat waiting: "They take their time because they are so incredibly sure of themselves. Selective Service, the FBI—the whole system is so smugly confident. *It really believes in itself!*"

Agent Hansen was the first to arrive from the Federal Bureau of Investigation. He came in white-faced, wearing a look that seemed to say, "What a breach of trust and good manners!" His investigator's glance took in an unusual scene: blood splattered on the floor, file cabinets yawning, two clergymen and two well-dressed laymen waiting composedly for arrest.

Therein began a relationship. The FBI, the Federal marshals, and the city police assumed that we were civilized men and that they were also. Our public standing and their training told them this, if our actions did not. Within or without jail, they would give us impersonal respect and consideration. It was good police-community relations. Nevertheless, the four of us were aware that implicit in their attitude was an acute sensitivity to our political potential. We had obviously made trouble for Selective Service and for the machinery of militarism which had begun this war and which kept it fueled. We could make trouble for them as well. Establishmentarianism had its benefits: We had a certain following and allegiance, and there was the ponderous and vaguely understood power of the Church, plus the volatile stridency of peace communities around the country.

In a word, we were bureaucrats who had acted out of context— but still bureaucrats. Their attitudes became more deferential when it came to me. In their eyes, a priest seemed to carry a certain aura about him which was never wholly extinguished by anything he might have done. The aura came partly from clerical totem, partly from deserved reputation, partly from establishment logic. And it won a regular response in taking care of alcoholic priests and in giving mild admonitions for traffic violations. It would win me care and courtesy, despite my messy variations of law-breaking.

Nonetheless, take these men from neutral ground, and they would revert to type—that is, they would protect the values and goals of the system. Their rationale is the "preservation of law and order," but they are unconsciously saying, "Our way of life must

survive!" To them, that is not a debatable issue. Had they been
on hand when we acted, they would probably have used any
means to stop us; or if escape had been the plan, they would have
pursued us relentlessly. All of which stems from the fact that life
remains reductively simple for most cops, and paradoxically, their
long hours in court, listening to testimony and giving it, does little
to convince them that it is complex for most others.

There was a quick hearing that afternoon at the Federal Commissioner's office—the machinery could turn over slow or fast, depending on the need. The Government, through the prosecution,
went into phase one of carrot and stick. It treated us now with
utmost leniency, knowing that it would sacrifice nothing in doing
so. Later, its position would improve, and it could treat us as it
willed. The U.S. District Attorney, a former Rhodes Scholar
named Stephen Sachs, offered us release on a personal recog-
nizance bond of one thousand dollars.

We refused to sign the bond, and refused again later at our
arraignment. Such a move was not idle heroics, as the Government
believed. It was merely an attempt to keep the initiative, to accept
consequences, to shun privilege, to avoid co-optation, and above
all to keep our consistency and integrity. Up to that point our only
voluntary suffering had been indecision, anguish over imponder-
ables, and the temporary shock of feeling very much alone. We
would be utterly unrealistic if we regarded these inconveniences
as notable counterpoints to the terrible drama of tribulation imposed by our country on the world. Our tiny diversion from
America's central business of war-making had to be continued and
given further meaning.

Resistance, we felt, did not terminate with one act or another.
It had to be pursued or dropped. In this case, pursuing it meant
using available nonviolent tools to challenge the fierce and systematic imposition of American myth, exploitation, and militarism
upon the weak and hopeless. Even as before, we had to ask ourselves what human response is necessary against the dehumanization of our society, with its mechanical surrogates, its overproduction and overconsumption, its contempt of marginal people, its
obsession with ideological excuses, its profound trust in force, its

fears and insecurities—all the sick hang-ups of a people who had too much and wanted too much more. One could disassociate from such ruinous preoccupations; one could choose exile from such a company; one could fast against its extravagance and decadence.

We went to jail and began to fast. The reactions were curious. What we had done remained unintelligible and threatening to most people, but to cap it off with a choice of jail and fasting compounded the insult. By letter and telegram, they loaded us with frightened invective and scorn; those at hand watched us anxiously for unpredictable or menacing acts. The warden of Baltimore City Jail isolated us from the other prisoners after asking if we felt belligerent or if we intended to disrupt his jail. The inspector of Federal prisons came up from Washington to gaze upon us with official apprehension and to inquire solicitously for our health and mental balance. The guards kept us under constant, nervous surveillance. We had to sleep in beds visible from the corridor, and if a shower or nature call took us out of sight, nothing would suffice but an on-the-scene inspection. Meantime, night and day, five huge ceiling lights helped with the watch.

We had apparently decided upon an indefinable course, employing weapons as devious as they were untouchable. Social value and code told our jailers, the Government, and the public at large that nobody chooses jail. Jail rather chooses somebody because he had not been leaven to the Great Society; because he had not, in fact, conformed to the gut need of the social monolith for faceless and anonymous service. Furthermore, nobody punished the stomach, unless perhaps he had an overweight problem or runaway metabolism. We had none of these ills, yet we perversely accepted only liquids for eight days. By the clock, orderlies brought us food; just as regularly, they took it back. Before we left jail, anxiety over our fast reached an absurd point—blood pressure and pulse tests were taken every four hours, even through the night. A few more days and they probably would have fed us intravenously.

Only the prisoners accepted what we were and what we were attempting to do. Many came to thank us with embarrassing friendliness and genuine emotion. Why accept us, why thank us?

These men, most of them black, had learned to recognize with unerring rectitude a human act and a human relationship, just as they unerringly recognized a superficial or false one. It came from not being offered any relationship, I suppose from not having anyone tell them, "You're a man, and I respect you for that! Period." They had foundered somewhere outside the Great American Dream, apparently helpless in the pit dug for them beneath our social ladders. And there they had learned priceless lessons, like responding to justice with justice, and giving love in answer to love. As their presence in jail suggested, they had not submitted to injustice and hate. One morning, several black orderlies were blamed without cause by the duty nurse. When they got the drift of her diatribe, they began to analyze her problems in classic vernacular. They had met her kind before; they recognized her injustice immediately; they knew how to resist and to educate her. She soon felt her helplessness, and later she called them together to apologize.

The counts against them were several, and they were administered with ruthless exactitude. To begin with, these men were black, and they were poor. Furthermore, they had not acted out their role; that is, they had not given grateful docility in exchange for existence in a white man's world. They had not bought what they could not buy and share. Somewhere along the line they had compared white rhetoric against black reality, and they found the rhetoric a lie and the reality an insult. In return, they had done the only thing they could do and keep their sanity—resist. Their resistance had taken humanly diverse and rich forms: numbers, drug addiction, alcoholism, burglary, confidence schemes, assault. All had different experiences, different stories; but all had the same conclusion: Theirs was a bum rap. And their meaning went deeper than their words.

Who could really disagree? The white world had conspired against them. The white world had decided that the only good nigger was a white man's nigger—a house nigger, Eldridge Cleaver called him.

Our brothers, as Tom Lewis called the black prisoners, sensed that their treatment was appallingly and psychotically wrong, and not even good for Whitey. Survival suggested many directions and many methods, but obviously Whitey's rules had to go, since Whitey lived them least of all. Whitey's whiteness, wealth, power, morality—all the fiercely held myth and status—had to go. These idols were tearing the world apart and could no longer be endured. Our brothers had mothers, aunts, and grandmothers who "toted" from white homes to compensate for the pittance received for cleaning, cooking, and raising white children. They had ancestor-soldiers like Crispus Attucks and Salem Poor, and rebels like Nat Turner. They came honestly by protest, and it signified little that protest was labeled crime by white man's law. White man's law said nothing about foreign slaughter, or having horror weapons and the will to use them, or letting people physically starve and spiritually die inside, or the profligacies and intrigues of economic royalists. White man's law had rationalized the rape of colored people for centuries, and now it seemed intent upon ruining the world for everybody. Who needed it?

A far more basic issue for them was that such a society—racist, hedonistic, brutal, incomparably arrogant—could no longer qualify as a human society. Lemminglike, it had chosen sadism, orgy, and the flag to the death. Moreover, death would come from its own internal rot, or it would come from the symbol of its defeat: the very bomb calculated to protect it. Meanwhile, its victims—who were at once its best wealth—would protest, would testify against it, would fill its antiwar parades, poor people's crusades, and jails, would pick its vegetables and fruit and struggle in its ghettos; and at the same time white, law-abiding, and rational men would woo its God, run its churches, businesses, and defense plants, would deliberate in its halls of law and decision, would send its young men to kill, and would fill up the cup of doom and death—perhaps to overflowing.

The security we felt with men like these was very nearly absolute. They bore the same marks of contempt and ostracism as the "publicans and sinners" with whom the Lord took company. Like them also, they had received the divine revelation entrusted to "little ones," and we were privileged to share it. We soon learned in jail something that had been slowly taught us through the years. They were the groaning masses favored by Christ, the people about whom Jefferson and Lincoln used to ruminate, the majority who against incredible misuse and betrayal had preserved more human integrity than their masters. They were the ones, we felt, who would have something more final to say about the future of man than the 'even then in the White House or the Rockefellers or the trustees of the multiversities.

Prison grapevines established the fact that we were there; newspapers and TV collaborated it. On our first Sunday in jail we took a seat with the other prisoners gathered for a 6 A.M. Eucharist. The chaplain told them that two war protestors would worship with them and that one was a priest. "Yeh," said one huge black man, "he's one of us!" I heard the remark, and it filled me with shame and something bordering on despair. Because the fact is that I had not been one of them, and was only learning gropingly that not being one of them was an inexcusable mistake. It was not even good tactics or politics, let alone good morality. In regard to the war, and indirectly in the cause of the poor, I had talked at length with Dean Rusk, corresponded with Robert McNamara and Walt Whitman Rostow, consulted with Senators like J. William Fulbright, Joseph Tydings, and Daniel Brewster, debated Congressmen, State Department representatives, and academic "experts" all over the country—all advocates of power or spokesmen for it. But any assumption that one must work with those who happen to have power, however they came by it or however they use it, is a fallacy offensive to both human integrity and to the democratic process. It is a myth communicated for popular consumption—and obedience.

Unfortunately for the advocates and spokesmen, power is justified by its source, its delegation, and its use. And in light of this, what have these men said to Vietnam *as it is* or to those who have to fight it and endure it or to the imperial ambition that caused it?

Stokely Carmichael, Huey Newton, Eldridge Cleaver, and the SDS kids, Camilo Torres, Che Guevara, Douglas Bravo, and the NLF were closer to truth and humanity than I, in the sense of fidelity to an imperative that sent them to the people and their cause. Their reason for doing so is neither subtle nor complicated;

they merely responded to situations of injustice too monumental
to be ignored. To them, justice is meaningless apart from the
struggle for the power belonging to the people, so that they might
have an adequate voice in their lives. According to them, the right
to power as a revolutionary weapon is more potent than the fact
of power. For when the right to power is scorned, the fact of
power becomes unjust. Finally, joining the people and standing
for their dignity is really to stand with the majority, a point that
decision-makers will angrily dispute. (The very obviousness of
that fact—two billion strong—makes it all the more dangerous in
their minds.)

To the Christian, they are "the people," not only because they
are the most of men, but because the Gospel gives them its staunch
approval—in the sense that their poverty and color saves them
from the inhuman failings of pride, avarice, and hypocrisy. The
Beatitudes strikingly bring this out, especially in Luke, who de-
scribes the Lord's view of humanity as directly opposite to the
view held by technological society. One is "happy" or "blessed"
for being poor, for being hungry, for having to weep now, for
being hated. Obviously, poverty, hunger, anguish of soul, and
being an object of hatred define the human condition. And one
can claim humanity only when one can claim them, or claim them
on behalf of others. Christ Himself was true to this view, not only
because He was a poor man and a servant of others, but because
He became most human in the criminality and despair of His
death. Only then could the favor of His Father rest fully upon
Him. Only then could He become fully MAN.

Christian justice does not demand confidence in the powers
that be, but confidence in the power of people, or power where it
ought to be. And since power does not reside sufficiently with
those whose human rights require it, divine power intercedes to
offer a timeless justice. "But God has chosen what the world regards as foolish to shame the wise, and what the world regards
as weak, God has chosen to shame the strong, and what the world
regards as low, contemptible, mere nothing, God has chosen to
bring to naught the things that are; so that no human being might
boast in his sight" (I Corinthians 1:26–29).

Violence is the last refuge of the incompetent.

—ISAAC ASIMOV

Peace is the mark of a civilized man, war the mark of a barbarian.

—MAHATMA GANDHI

The United States must further Western control of 'much needed rice, rubber, and tin.' . . . Perhaps even more important would be the psychological effect of the fall of Indochina. It would be taken by many as a sign that the force of Communism is ir-reversible and would lead to an attitude of defeatism. [Therefore,] Communist forces must be decisively conquered down to the last pocket of resistance.

—U.S. STATE DEPARTMENT RELEASE, 1951

It is a fair contention, I think, to maintain that a sobering per-centage of Americans, including leading industrialists and policy-makers, would have no difficulty reconciling the above statements. They would find in them neither contradiction nor abuse in foreign policy. A high official in Washington once told me blandly but sincerely, "This Government is intent upon peace. We desire nothing for ourselves; we denounce hatred and violence. It is others who choose them." I listened incredulously, and with a nausea that I could hardly control. We kept up the niceties of respect for one another, but somehow we were beyond the point of discussion.

Which goes to say that those who direct our country's course, plus those who support it, believe in their competence, dedication to peace, and qualities of civilization, *plus* the means taken to achieve peace and civilization for others. Civilization equals peace, they say, but civilization becomes impossible unless it is capitalist and "free world"—in other words, American. In effect, this is an-other way of saying that we reserve the right to conduct the world's business and to engineer its politics, so that from these indisputable blessings our peace and civilization might introduce the new millennium. Look at West Germany, they say, or Japan, Thailand, Venezuela, and the Union of South Africa. They learned, and look at them now; they are civilized, peaceful, free-world allies.

To state the case of official power so baldly is not to denigrate it as purely evil, not to nullify its accomplishments, not to claim that it conspires to run the world. American power is as humanitarian as its people. It does want to help others to a better life; it does recognize the right of other nations to chart their internal course. But it does question their doing it as they choose. And above all, it opposes their right to do so *if* that right interferes with American interests. In a word, one can forgive our leaders for believing that the United States has the best of all possible economic and political systems; but one cannot overlook their failure to bring reality close to rhetoric. Their failure to deal with self-determination—in our ghettos and reservations, in the bleak shacks of our rural poor, in the rice paddies of Vietnam, and in the foothills of the Andes—constitutes their fatal flaw.

The historical premises that established both our national life-style and our foreign empire have received more extensive treatment in prior chapters of this book. The reader will forgive a cursory return to them, for the simple reason that they compose a consistent, entrenched, institutionalized theme that is now central to the tragedy of our domestic and foreign policy.

American commercialism, even prior to our Revolution, owed its philosophy to men like John Locke and Oliver Cromwell, and its theology to Puritan Calvinism. Locke, for example, maintained that property was a right which preceded the state's right to exist, and he asserted that "the supreme power cannot take from any man any part of his property without his own consent." [1] In turn, Cromwell and Henry Ireton said that "only freeholders constituted the body politic, and they could use their property [land] as they pleased, uncontrolled by obligations to any superior, or by the need of consulting the mass of men, who were mere tenants at will, with no fixed interest or share in the land of the kingdom." [2]

For its own part, Puritanism incessantly stressed the duties of stewardship in God's vineyard, the success or ill-success of which won or lost for the believer the name of Christian, and won or lost him his salvation. R. H. Tawney speaks of seventeenth-century Puritanism, which gave a theological base to the capitalism taught by Locke:

Not sufficiency to the needs of daily life, but limitless increase and expansion, became the goal of the Christian's efforts. Not consumption, on which the eyes of earlier sages had been turned, but production, became the pivot of his argument. . . . For the world exists not to be enjoyed, but to be conquered. Only its conqueror deserves the name Christian. For such a philosophy, the question "What shall it profit a man?" carries no sting. In winning the world, he wins the salvation of his own soul as well.[3]

James Madison, an immediate witness of the liabilities of our early commercial spirit, wrote tartly to Thomas Jefferson in 1786: "A continuance of the present anarchy of our commerce will be a continuance of the unfavorable balance on it, which by draining us of our metals . . . [will bring our ruin]. In fact, most of our political evils may be traced up to our commerical ones, and most of our moral to our political."[4] And Edward Everett spoke as aptly to our times as to his own in saying that expansion was the "*principle* of our institutions."[5]

It is not surprising that the spirit of empire derived from the spirit of commerce, nor that a tiny and weak federation of states, newly emerged into freedom, already thought of itself as an empire. So profoundly aggressive was our business sense, and so naturally did our sense of empire flow from it, that within fifty years from our foundation we could fight the British to a standstill in the War of 1812 and achieve our desires west of the Mississippi after the armistice; we could secure from Spain, without war, an immense territory stretching from the Gulf of Mexico to the Pacific; and we could, through the Monroe Doctrine of 1823, claim primary economic rights over the whole Western Hemisphere. This was no mean accomplishment for a fledgling nation, one might venture, and not entirely accidental.

The crisis of the 1890's began a historic trend of economic reevaluations as regular as the intermittent recessions causing them. By 1894 unemployment had seized four million men, Coxey's

Army had completed its pitiful march, and besides the tragic Pullman strike, there were thirty others of major proportions. Financial and industrial life came to a virtual halt, but from the economic stagnation arose a kind of do-or-die debate as to new directions for the nation. In utterly logical fashion, the debate centered on the best way to expand, not whether expansion ought to be the rule. And there was *no* disagreement that expansion ought to be overseas.

As a concurrent development, the crisis of 1890 marked the demise of the famed American entrepreneur whose brash frontiersmanship had characterized our economic style. The corporation rose to prominence; it was more efficient. In the meantime, Grover Cleveland came to be known as our first serious "Manifest Destiny" President. More than any other leader of his time, Cleveland outlined in broad framework the imperial nature of America's foreign policy.

Crisis can be expected to bring to the national rhetoric a quality of honesty somewhat lacking at other times. Inevitably, when the nation's business has stagnated, bringing in its train unemployment, collective anxiety, and social disruption, our leaders have spoken with a frankness that we ought to find illuminating. Senator Albert J. Beveridge, for example, addressed both the crisis of 1890 and the essence of the American economy when he said in April, 1897: "American factories are making more than the American people can use; American soil is producing more than they can consume. Fate has written our policy for us; the trade of the world must and shall be ours." [6] During the same period, the critical nature of which produced our fateful Open Door policy, its author, Secretary of State John Hay, said this in 1899: "In the field of trade and commerce, we shall be the keen competitors of the richest and greatest powers, and they need no warning to be assured that in that struggle, we shall bring the sweat to their brows." [7] President William McKinley concluded during the Cuban crisis in 1897 that other nations had obligations to keep us prosperous, a conclusion not far removed from the premises of expansionism themselves. Writing to his new minister to Spain in July, 1897, he explained the reason for coming to this con-

clusion: "The chronic condition of trouble . . . causes disturbance
in the social and political condition of our own peoples. . . . A
continuous irritation within our own borders injuriously affects
the normal function of business, and tends to delay the condition
of prosperity to which this country is entitled." [8]

Again, Theodore Roosevelt, who openly admitted that he had
helped force our intervention in Cuba, said this in his Presidential
Message of December, 1901:

Business concerns which have the largest means at their disposal . . .
take the lead in the strife for commercial supremacy among the nations
of the world. America has only just begun to assume the commanding
position in the international business world which we believe will be
more and more hers. It is of the utmost importance that this position be
not jeopardized, especially at a time when the overflowing abundance
of our own natural resources and the skill, business energy, and mechanical aptitude of our people make foreign markets essential.[9]

And Woodrow Wilson, who combined the attributes of idealism
and pragmatism to an unusual degree, said this at a campaign
dinner in 1912: "We have reached, in short, a critical point in the
process of our prosperity. It has now become a question with us
whether it shall continue or shall not continue. . . . We need
foreign markets, [because] our domestic market is too small." [10]

One need not go on to labor the point. Our economic upswing
has continued from Wilson's time with minor and major fluctua-
tions, until we now make a fair pretense of doing the world's business. In our time the Truman Doctrine has updated John Hay's
Open Door policy and has been in turn updated by the synthesis
of Walt Whitman Rostow—what critics have euphemistically
described as "rollback" policy. The United States is not exactly a
fortress or a garrison which has armed itself to fight off its enemies.
Nor is our world role exactly a police one. We are an empire on
the offensive, simply because our economy, with its perpetual state
of disequilibrium, *requires* an offensive to keep it from larger un-
balance and from falling on its face.

One evening, while participating in some local Congressional
hearings on Vietnam, a State Department economist challenged
me with this difficulty: "Father, I am surprised that you subscribe

to the theory that competitive economics are a root cause of war. That theory has been declared obsolete long ago." When I recovered from my amazement and asked him why it should be obsolete, he could not answer to my satisfaction or to that of the audience. His failure that evening might spring from the fact that an economy cannot survive if its economists condemn it in the abstract. Quite simply, our friend shared the system and profited from it. And because he did, he found no need to alter it or to do other than justify it.

I can feel pity for his problem without becoming part of it. The fact is, however, that a nation as relatively unpopulous as our own cannot be as rich as we are without being party to injustice that staggers the mind. The fact is, also, that we can choose to ignore or to excuse our colossal wealth without sharing it, but the rest of the world chooses neither to ignore it nor to excuse it. And the rest of the world must be considered. "The rest of the world—Ah! there is the rub." [11]

National greed does not differ essentially from personal greed. Understandably, both are unpopular subjects with nations or individuals guilty of them. Nor does the nature of greed change because it is syndicated under the corporate names of some of our industrial giants.

Still more unpopular as subject matter is a discussion of what we will do to keep our wealth and increase it. In other words, our greed is measured by the methods employed to give it efficiency and conviction—the methods of the cold war: arms sales and military giveaways of 46.3 billion dollars since 1949; mutual defense treaties with forty-two nations; military and economic aid to nearly one hundred others; war costs involving three-quarters of every tax dollar; Vietnam expenditures of nearly 40 billion dollars annually, and another 60 billion dollars in available "defense" appropriations; military allocations from Congress exceeding Defense Department requests; Pentagon control of approximately the same proportion of all Federal property (53 per cent, or 183 billion dollars worth) as the proportion of the world's productive capacity under U.S. control; a per capita nuclear equivalent of fifteen tons of TNT for every living person, with proportionate back-up capacities of bacteriological and chemical weapons; and military interventions, outposts, or intelligence activities in Vietnam, the Dominican Republic, Guatemala, Thailand, Laos, Bolivia, Honduras, and Peru.

By a logic entirely straightforward and purposeful, our economy leaves in its train the same foreign and domestic poverty. It cross-seminates itself both abroad and at home, flourishing off a victim class, and indeed, producing one. It takes its profits from a starving world and refuses to release the poor in the United States from their poverty, for they are too lucrative an element. Even as it is in the world, inequity of income in the United States is the most sinister and explosive of social facts. No income shift favoring the poor has taken place in the nation since 1945, and it took place then because of ten million men in uniform and because of the manpower demands in war industry. The Citizen Board of Inquiry into Hunger and Malnutrition in the United States found that 10,764,000 Americans suffer from hunger, and that 20,000,000 more suffer from malnutrition. By way of contrast, Fortune guessed that Howard Hughes and Paul Getty are probably billionaires, 6 others are worth at least half a billion dollars, and 153 individuals are worth in excess of 100 million dollars.

The graduated income tax is supposed to equalize incomes, but it often fails miserably to do so. The rich find loopholes for themselves or lobby until they get them. A taxpayer earning less than five thousand dollars has a tax rate of about 14 per cent, whereas those earning in excess of fifty thousand dollars have a rate of about 25 per cent. To stress that disparity still more, there is the claim of Representative Henry Reuss of Wisconsin that "a significant number of millionaires and multimillionaires escape taxation entirely." According to him, in 1962 three multimillionaires who earned more than five million dollars annually paid nothing, and in 1965 thirty-five men who earned more than half a million dollars paid nothing.

The rich who pay less than their share—or nothing—and the poor who pay more than theirs and starve—this is what unrest in America is all about. The top fifth in our society gets 45.5 per cent of the national income; the bottom fifth gets 5 per cent. Or to juggle inequity a bit differently to allow time for absorption: The top 5 per cent of the nation gets 20 per cent of the income; the bottom 20 per cent gets 5 per cent.[12]

One need no longer speculate about 1984 coming. It is upon us. The "rationality" of our national purpose, our technology, our economic acumen, our libertarianism, and our morality has ended in an irrationality that has set the world afire, and which fans the blaze enthusiastically. In fact, the irrationality is so widely denied, so subtly excused, so profoundly entrenched, so self-reinforcing, that few who understand it imagine that it can be controlled or changed peaceably.

The malaise goes deeper still. It hits rock bottom in the failure to realize that affluence asks a greater price than the ambiguous effort of earning it—the price of tending it like a menial, of living within its limits, of extenuating its responsibilities, and of choosing an unreal world. Affluence makes absurd the hope of becoming human. Anyone within its grip can do little but harm himself and others.

With affluence fashioning the nation's culture and directing its purpose, it is not surprising that technology collaborates with the Government in controls that are more subtle and pervasive than those of an oligarchy. It is not surprising that Christianity conducts itself not as Gospel community, but as an ethical management system under a trivial veneer of rubric and ritual. It is not surprising that a style of life emerges which Americans accept un-critically and evangelize with ingenuous goodwill—a style of life which includes redoubtable productive genius, unimaginable mili-tary might, moralistic fervor, and the staunch belief that peace and plenty will be our gifts to the world—or they will not come at all.

When evidence to the contrary appears, it is ignored or it is hotly contested. The result is our inability to dissent or to make dissent felt; our unwillingness to secure world and domestic peace by sacrificing personal, group, and national interests; our reluc-tance to admit that the poor solidify the middle class and make the rich richer; our compulsion to rely on the "higher reality" of religion to escape the lower.

What can be said of our style of life except that it resembles
the corruption and decadence of empire? If it be that, it may be
in the throes of imperial decline and fall, whose hopeful side will
be a revolution to build a better nation and a better world, or
whose tragic side will be domestic and international anarchy that
will lead the world into nuclear firestorm and human collapse.

Friends recently returned from Rome—correspondents, superiors, priests—tell me of the anxious uncertainty affecting almost
everyone there. When I ask what the uncertainty is about, answers invariably narrow down to a couple: not knowing what
needs to be said and not knowing what needs to be done. Where-
upon, I ask if the Vatican, bishops, and theologians have any
grasp of how the Church is to serve man better under poverty,
war, racism, nationalism, and what have you. Some friends answer—tentatively, theoretically—but confusion reigns as to whether
the Church *should* stand with man in his tragic circumstance, and
whether it *can* stand with man. Then I ask if it is not just as it is
here at home. Yes, they admit sadly. This in my opinion makes
the dilemma triple-headed: Is the Church for itself? Or is it for
man? And if it is for itself, how can it be for man?

A few years ago, when Church authorities exiled my Jesuit
brother to Latin America for his peace work, another priest expressed outrage at his treatment: "It is impossible to be a Christian in this Church!" His outburst, however well-intentioned, was
not exactly to the point. However regressive and pompous the
Church might be, to hold it responsible for a climate in which
pure Christian witness cannot flourish is as foolhardy (untheologi-
cal) as expecting it to mass-produce Christians of the pure variety.
If one can qualify as a Christian—and one never does this fully—
it is both because and in spite of the Church, which has ingeni-
ously shared both Christ's bed and the world's throughout history.
It is both a bride and a whore, like all of us.

Beyond such comments, a great deal more probing is necessary.
Otherwise, one tends toward unfair and even dangerous general-
ization. Somewhat more helpful to me is reflection on our immedi-

ate past—before World War II—when the Church fulfilled a need for Catholics. Life then was something of a local struggle, simple and relatively placid. The world had not begun to impinge on religious and national life with its strident demands and complexities. Consequently, there was no basis for comparison, one accepted without question a format of life purified by time, authority, and experience, doing the best possible with it and being responsible toward it.

In those days, so deceptively serene and wholesome, what alternatives were there to parochial-school education, to job, college, or religious life after high school? Or when national crisis approached, what else did one do except the decent and just thing by entering military service against monsters like Hitler and Tojo? If one did not know why one acted, one nonetheless knew what to do, simply because both Church and State told one. And there was no contradiction and no confusion between their respective recommendations.

World War II destroyed that life-style forever. It suggested, moreover, a most threatening possibility: that both the nation-state and the institutional Church were obsolete and doomed. Men came to realize, when they thought about it, that neither seemed capable of avoiding or limiting the slaughter and ruin of the war years. Men realized further that both institutions might have been mainly responsible for the war: the nation-state by its adherence to national interest, the Church by its curious allegiance to the nation-state. Furthermore, the Vatican contributed to eventual collapse by supporting the Church hierarchies of both the Allied and the Axis powers while promulgating its classic condemnations of total war to the world.

Despite the obstacle presented by their allegiance to Church and State, the war freed men for distinct choices—atomic destruction or world family. It "freed" them not to any universal extent, but in a vanguard of thought and compassion which saw the issue precisely for what it was: Man would once again allow international tensions to gather to a point of fury—to nuclear war, this time—or he would control them through new and more humane institutions.

A PUNISHMENT FOR PEACE

Before long, however, it appeared to those gambling on a human future that the struggle had become despairingly unequal. All the residues of human fear, greed, and national pride seemed to gather strength from the war years. The end of one war became hope for peace, but it also became an excuse to start another one. The cold war began. Nationalism throughout the world received a raucous example from the hypernationalism of the great powers. Technology settled on a course of arming mankind with conventional and atomic weapons. The starving and powerless were isolated in the white "have" world, and despite the American-Soviet rivalry, the great powers stood together against the Third World. Colored expectations and pride spread in the "have-not" world from Africa to ghetto America to Southeast Asia, taking the form of political autonomy, representation in the United Nations, civil-rights movements, riots, and wars of national liberation. And as usual, the powerful sought the *status quo* while the poor sought freedom.

Almost predictably, the Church took the side of power. Although Rome spoke with declining authority and/or condemnations of war, poverty, racism, and nationalism, it did nothing to undermine its status as a "free world" capitalist institution with vast international assets and finances. It did little to analyze or to protest the "balance of power" between the superpowers, their efforts to divide the world, or the frustration of those efforts through nuclear stalemate. It did little to instruct its national bodies in the priorities of Catholicism, priorities in the international order which stood over and beyond local preoccupations. One can suspect the reason—institutional survival and unity in preference to identification with peace and freedom movements. And the basic fallacy of such a policy lay in the belief that the Church could survive without having a real hand in the survival of mankind.

In a very real sense, national church bodies remain faithful to the same aims within their countries. They either toil to improve the efficiency of their management, or they pursue a liberal course of "renewal" by challenging Rome on issues like birth control or celibacy, or they display concern for the secular order by reflecting the social aims of the state and supporting its programs. Habitually, the Church is conservative; at the best it is reformist; almost never is it revolutionary.

In any case, or whatever the course pursued, the Church is a bureaucracy, and it acts like one. This means that it limits the human choices of its subjects, even as other bureaucracies do. These limitations or controls are familiar and well tested: emolument, position, power, security, and fear. Some of them entice; some of them pressure. But whatever their nature, they place the subject in a position where he is more reluctant to face the injustice of his Church than to face an issue and to take an unpopular public stand. How many priests have there been who would rather go to jail on a question of public morality than risk reprisal from Church officialdom? They do nothing, and nothing is done to them. They neither favor justice publicly, nor do they go to jail, nor are they punished by the Church. In effect, they have defaulted on their Christianity, their priesthood, and their manhood. They have played the game of power—not, however, as its patron, but as its victim.

The Christian who takes both Gospel and democracy seriously thus finds himself open on two fronts. He must fight the opaque and arrogant power of both the Church and the State. And for anyone to be scandalized by that assertion or made apprehensive is to imply failure in observation, experience, and conviction. All tell one that the integral bureaucracies of a technocracy are an alliance—corporate bedfellows, if you will—whose peculiar wisdom of power has brought the world to the brink of ruin.

One takes off the blinders, so to speak, and one strips away the illusions. The point of life is to come to terms with life in all its diversity—its richness, promise, insecurity, and sometimes brutality. To serve human life today is to unmask it when it is inhuman, to enrich it when it is poor, to win it justice when it is crushed, to give it peace under conflict, to love it in all cases and circumstances. This is no more than joining the human race and serving the Church, particularly when the Church sees real Christians and real Christian communities as its greatest enemies.

The Church is in the way, someone has said; it is the moral

custodian of the *status quo,* and therefore it is a power that
honors the conventional signs of privilege—wealth, racism, war. It
is not for self-determination, either personal or international; it is
not for revolution, even when revolution is justifiable and nonviolent; it is not for justice and not against injustice. It is rather
for its ooolooilul oolf, which is to say that it serves life on its own
terms, molding man to its own pretentious pattern or taking him
not at all—a process somewhat similar, one might reflect, to our
Government's effort to make Southeast Asian Americans out of
Vietnamese peasants.

The institutional Church rarely speaks of its real values; it
does so only when it feels itself threatened, or when it has been
thrown off guard and into crisis. Apparently, it spoke of its real
values when we symbolically used blood against the draft files
in Baltimore. One can be grateful for the honesty employed in
labeling our act "flamboyant," "bizarre," "self-defeating," and in
reference to myself, "compromising to his priestly ministry." But
one suspects nonetheless that the vigorous repugnance and dis-
association expressed by the official Church, in contrast to its
silence over the genocide in Vietnam, is far more betraying than
anything we or our sympathizers can say.

It is far more betraying, in fact, than the petulant indictments
of a Charles Davis or a James Kavanaugh, whose concern for
conscience and its abuse within the Church led them not at all to
stand exposed on the great public issues, where the *real* conflicts
lie. In any event, a new axiom has developed. "Let the Church
speak officially, and make a public showing of slipper in mouth."
One of my superiors remarked with relish that I would have to
"bear the full consequences of the law." Having failed to educate
me, he was now ceding the privilege to the Government and its
law.

Nevertheless, we are grateful for honesty, for without it one
is taken off balance, and true positions can hardly be known. If
anything, reactions against one by the Church and the Government broaden the scope of one's responsibility, not only by speaking of values and covenants within the establishment, but by
speaking of the people who hold them. By forcing them into the

lists of dialogue and even of conflict, one does about all one can do for them. For their position allows them human options too few in number, and in giving them a few more, one helps to give them a little more chance to be human. They, too, have a right to the mercy of the Lord and to the justice and love of men.

I write this from jail, which the Government uses to protect society from us. (We say that jail also protects us from society.) At any rate, because we demonstrated again in Catonsville, Maryland, on May 17, our sentence on May 24 for the blood-pouring incident is six years, and though conviction and sentence are under appeal, the courts allow us no bail. Finally, Catonsville assures us of both Federal and state charges, with maximum penalties of fifty-four years. As the Scripture says, "It is an awful thing to fall into the hands of the living Government"—pardon me—"God." Judicial overkill, somebody called it.

As for the Church, let it not be found lacking. I have been formally relieved of my parish duties and informally relieved of my faculties in the Archdiocese of Baltimore. The latter was done without charges, without a hearing, without notification. It is unofficial suspension of a unilateral kind, which leads me to prefer the tender mercies of the courts. But I must admit that as a priest, I find it particularly painful, since I can no longer offer the Eucharist with the prisoners nor discuss the Scripture with them nor hear their confessions.

Yet understanding does not fail, nor does contentment and peace. If the purposes of Christ are to be fulfilled through their ironies, then let it be so. And if one is to be used in their fulfillment, let that be so. For myself, it is privilege enough, and gain enough.

EPILOGUE

(The following is a press statement released by the undersigned on the occasion described below.)

Today, May 17, 1968 we enter Local Board #33, Catonsville, Maryland, to seize the Selective Service records and to burn them outside with homemade napalm. (The recipe for napalm we took from the Special Forces Handbook, published by the Army's School of Special Warfare at Ft. Bragg, North Carolina.)

As American citizens, we have worked with the poor in the ghetto and abroad. In the course of our Christian ministry, we have watched our country produce more victims than an army of us could console or restore. Two of us face immediate sentencing for similar acts against Selective Service. All of us identify with the victims of American oppression all over the world. We submit voluntarily to their involuntary fate.

We use napalm on these draft records because napalm has burned people to death in Vietnam, Guatemala, and Peru; and because it may be used in America's ghettos. We destroy these draft records not only because they exploit our young men, but because these records represent misplaced power, concentrated in the ruling class of America. Their power threatens the peace of the world; it isolates itself from public dissent and manipulates parliamentary process. And it reduces young men to a cost-efficiency item through the draft. In effect—if not in intent—the rulers of the United States want their global wars fought as cheaply as possible.

Above all, our protest attempts to illustrate why our country is torn at home and harassed abroad by enemies of its own creation. For a long time the United States has been an empire, and today it is history's richest nation. Representing 6 per cent of the world's people, our country controls half the world's productive capacity and two-thirds of its finance. It holds Northern and Southern America in an economic vise. In fifteen years time, economists think that its industry in Europe will be the third greatest industrial power in the world, after the United States and the Soviet Union. Our foreign profits run substantially higher than domestic profits. So industry flees abroad under Government patronage and protection from the CIA, counter-insurgency, and conflict management teams.

The military participates with economic and political sectors to form a triumvirate of power which sets and enforces policy. With an annual budget of more than 80 billion dollars, our military now controls over half of all Federal property (53 per cent, or 183 billion dollars) while U.S. nuclear and conventional weaponry exceeds that of the whole remaining world.

Peace negotiations with the North Vietnamese have begun in Paris. With other Americans, we hope a settlement will be reached, thus sparing the Vietnamese a useless prolongation of their suffering. However, this alone will not solve our nation's problems. The Vietnam war could end tomorrow and leave undisturbed the quality of our society, and its world role. Thailand, Laos, and the Dominican Republic have already been Vietnams. Guatemala, the Canal Zone, Bolivia, and Peru could be Vietnams overnight. Meanwhile, the colonies at home rise in rage and destructiveness. Our black people have concluded that after 350 years, their human acceptance is long overdue.

Injustice is the great catalyst of revolution. A nation that found life in revolution has now become the world's foremost counter-revolutionary force, not because the American people would have it that way, but because an expanding economy and continuing profits require an insistence on the *status quo*. Competitive capitalism as a system, and capitalists in general, must learn the hard lessons of justice, or a country may be swept away and humanity with it.

We believe that some property has no right to exist. Hitler's gas ovens, Stalin's concentration camps, atomic-bacteriological-chemical weaponry, files of conscription, and slum properties have no right to exist. When people starve for bread and lack decent housing, it is usually because the rich debase themselves with abuse of property, causing extravagance on their part and oppression and misery in others.

We are Catholic Christians who take the Christian Gospel seriously. We hail the recent Papal encyclical, *The Development of Peoples*. Quotes like the following give us hope:

No one is justified in keeping for his exclusive use what he does not need, when others lack necessities.

A revolutionary uprising—save where there is open, manifest, and long-standing tyranny which does great damage to fundamental personal rights and dangerous harm to the common good of the country—produces new injustices, throws more elements out of balance, and brings on new disasters.

It is a question of building a world where every man, no matter what his race, religion, or nationality, can live a fully human life, freed from slavery imposed on him by other men or natural forces, a world where the poor man Lazarus can sit down at the same table with the rich man.

The hour for action has now sounded. At stake are the survival of so many children and so many families overcome by misery, with no access to conditions fit for human beings; at stake are the peace of the world and the future of civilization.

Despite such stirring words, we confront the Catholic Church, other Christian bodies, and the synagogues of America with their silence and cowardice in the face of our country's crimes. We are convinced that the religious bureaucracy in this country is racist, guilty of complicity in war, and hostile to the poor. In utter fidelity to our faith, we indict religious leaders and their followers for their failure to serve our country and mankind.

Finally, we are appalled by the ruse of the American ruling

class invoking pleas for "law and order" to mask and perpetuate injustice. Let our President and the pillars of society speak of "law and justice" and back up their words with deeds. Then there will be "order." We have pleaded spoken, marched, and nursed the victims of this injustice. Now this injustice must be faced, and this we intend to do, with whatever strength of mind, body, and grace that God will give us. May He have mercy on our nation.

Rev. Daniel Berrigan
Rev. Philip Berrigan
Bro. David Darst
John Hogan
Thomas Lewis
Majorie Bradford Melville
Thomas Melville
George Mische
Mary Moylan

NOTES

CHAPTER II

[1] Eric Williams, quoted in Lerone Bennett, Jr., *Before the Mayflower: A History of the Negro in America 1619–1962* (Chicago: Johnson Publishing Co., 1962), p. 46.

[2] W. E. B. DuBois, quoted *ibid.*, p. 47.

[3] Harriet Beecher Stowe, quoted *ibid.*, p. 49.

[4] Stanley M. Elkins, quoted *ibid.*, p. 71.

[5] Fredcrick Douglass, quoted in Lerone Bennett, Jr., *The Negro Mood* (Chicago: Johnson Publishing Co., 1964), p. 64.

[6] Quoted in Bennett, *Before the Mayflower*, p. 169.

[7] *Ibid.*, p. 238.

[8] For an intriguing and exhaustive treatment of the subject, see Ronald Segal's *Race War* (New York: The Viking Press, Inc., 1966).

[9] Frantz Fanon, *Wretched of the Earth*, trans. by Constance Farrington (New York: Grove Press, Inc., 1965), pp. 252–255.

CHAPTER III

[1] Lerone Bennett, Jr., *Confrontation: Black and White* (Baltimore: Penguin Books, Inc., 1965), p. 38.

[2] Quoted in the editorial "Blow-up in the Cities," *The New Republic*, August 5, 1967, p. 5.

[3] See *I. F. Stone's Weekly*, July 25, 1966, p. 2.

[4] *Ibid.*, September 19, 1966.

[5] An idea propounded by W. H. Ferry in his paper *Black Colonies: A*

Final Solution, prepared for the Center for the Study of Democratic Institutions (Box 4068, Santa Barbara, Calif. 93103).

[6] For a fuller treatment, Anthony Towne's magnificent article "Revolution and the Marks of Baptism" in *Katallagete* (Box 430, Berea College Station, Berea, Ky. 40403) should be read.

[7] Whitney M. Young, Jr., *To Be Equal* (New York: McGraw Hill Book Company, 1964), p. 254.

CHAPTER IV

[1] Cordell Hull, quoted in William Appleman Williams, *The Tragedy of American Diplomacy* (New York: Dell Publishing Co., Inc., 1962), p. 162.

[2] William McGaffin and Darwin Knoll, "The White House Lies," *Progressive,* September, 1967, p. 17.

[3] See *ibid.,* p. 14.

[4] See the editorial in the Baltimore *News American,* January 14, 1968.

[5] Sen. Clifford Case, quoted in Maurice J. Goldbloom, "The Fulbright Revolt," *Commentary,* September, 1966.

[6] See Carl Oglesby and Richard Shaull, *Containment and Change* (New York: The Macmillan Co., 1967), p. 49.

[7] See *ibid.,* p. 50.

[8] See William Appleman Williams, *The Shaping of American Diplomacy* (Chicago: Rand McNally & Co., 1956), pp. 217–224.

[9] William Frye, quoted in Williams, *Tragedy of American Diplomacy,* p. 26.

[10] Woodrow Wilson, Columbia University Lectures (April, 1907), quoted *ibid.,* p. 66.

[11] Oglesby and Shaull, p. 62.

[12] Woodrow Wilson, quoted in Williams, *Tragedy of American Diplomacy,* p. 66.

[13] Woodrow Wilson, quoted *ibid.*

[14] William Redfield, quoted *ibid.,* p. 78.

[15] William Jennings Bryan, quoted *ibid.,* pp. 78–79.

[16] Raymond Robins, quoted *ibid.,* pp. 82–83.

[17] See Oglesby and Shaull, p. 66.

[18] Francis B. Sayre, in U.S., Dept. of State, *Commercial Policy Series, 1934–41.*

[19] Franklin D. Roosevelt, *Public Papers and Addresses,* comp. and collated by Samuel I. Rosenman, Vol. IV: *The Court Disapproves, 1935* (New York: Random House, Inc., 1938), p. 463.

[20] Lyndon B. Johnson, quoted in the Baltimore *Sun*, June 28, 1967.
[21] See Richard J. Barber, "The New Partnership," *The New Republic*, August 13, 1966.
[22] *Ibid.*, p. 17.
[23] See Richard Whalen, "Who Owns America?" *Saturday Evening Post*, December 30, 1967.
[24] See Joseph D. Phillips, "The Dollar Invades Europe," *The Nation*, September 18, 1967.
[25] *Time*, December 29, 1967, p. 56.
[26] See *ibid.*, p. 59.
[27] Alain Peyrefitte, quoted in Phillips, "The Dollar Invades Europe."
[28] John Gerassi, *The Great Fear in Latin America* (rev. ed.; New York: The Macmillan Co., 1965), p. 355.
[29] Harry Magdoff, "Rationalizing the Irrational," *The Nation*, September 18, 1967.
[30] See Appendix D in Seymour Melman, *Our Depleted Society* (New York: Holt, Rinehart and Winston, Inc., 1965).
[31] D. A. Fitzgerald, quoted in Melman, p. 150.
[32] Wayne Morse, quoted *ibid.*

CHAPTER V

[1] Harry S Truman, quoted in William Appleman Williams, *The Tragedy of American Diplomacy* (New York: Dell Publishing Co., Inc., 1962), p. 204.
[2] Max Born, "What Is Left to Hope For?" *Bulletin of the Atomic Scientists*, April, 1964, p. 2.
[3] *Ibid.*
[4] See Fred J. Cook, *The Warfare State* (New York: The Macmillan Co., 1962), p. 67.
[5] Sumner Welles, quoted in Carl Oglesby and Richard Shaull, *Containment and Change* (New York: The Macmillan Co., 1967), p. 35.
[6] For an incisive and fascinating survey of these years, see *ibid.*, pp. 33–45.
[7] G. L. Arnold, quoted in Williams, p. 210.
[8] Joseph Stalin, quoted *ibid.*, pp. 212–213.
[9] See Oglesby and Shaull, p. 44.
[10] Quoted in Williams, p. 232.
[11] William L. Clayton, quoted *ibid.*, p. 234.
[12] George C. Marshall, quoted in Gar Alperovitz, "Why We Dropped the Bomb," *Progressive*, August, 1965, p. 12.

[13] Harry S Truman, quoted *ibid.*
[14] Dwight D. Eisenhower, quoted *ibid.*
[15] William D. Leahy, quoted *ibid.*
[16] Curtis LeMay, quoted *ibid.*, pp. 10 10
[17] Winston Churchill, quoted *ibid.*, p. 13.
[18] Vannevar Bush, quoted *ibid.*
[19] J. Robert Oppenheimer, quoted *ibid.*, p. 23.
[20] Quoted *ibid.*, p. 14.
[21] J. Robert Oppenheimer, "The Control of Atomic Energy," *Foreign Affairs*, January, 1948.
[22] Bernard M. Baruch (June 16, 1946), quoted in Williams, p. 266.
[23] Henry A. Wallace (September, 1946), quoted *ibid.*
[24] George F. Kennan, quoted *ibid.*, p. 269.
[25] *Ibid.*, p. 274.
[26] Abraham Lincoln, quoted in Herbert Mitgang, "The Mexican War Dove," *The New Republic*, February 11, 1967.

CHAPTER VI

[1] John Locke, quoted in R. H. Tawney, *Religion and the Rise of Capitalism* (New York: Mentor Books, 1954), p. 214.
[2] Oliver Cromwell and Henry Ireton, quoted *ibid.*
[3] *Ibid.*, p. 206.
[4] James Madison, quoted in William Appleman Williams, *The Tragedy of American Diplomacy* (New York: Dell Publishing Co., Inc., 1962), p. 16.
[5] Edward Everett, quoted *ibid.*, p. 20.
[6] Albert J. Beveridge, quoted *ibid.*, p. 17.
[7] John M. Hay, quoted *ibid.*, pp. 17–18.
[8] William McKinley, quoted *ibid.*, p. 34.
[9] Theodore Roosevelt, quoted *ibid.*, p. 57.
[10] Woodrow Wilson, quoted *ibid.*, p. 67.
[11] Franklin D. Roosevelt (1936), quoted *ibid.*, p. 160.
[12] See "T.R.B. from Washington," *The New Republic*, May 11, 1968.